Advance Praise for *Customer Tells*

"Armed with the chimerical ability to thoroughly read a person's mind, opportunities would abound. Although this book won't provide you ESP, it comes very close. *Customer Tells* teaches a powerful and systematic approach to quickly assimilate crucial information from people and enables you to respond with prescience. Assiduous application of the outstanding knowledge of this book will make you a far, far better salesperson or client servicer. *Customer Tells* is a must read for anyone who desires to improve their interactions with people."

> — R. Todd Ruppert, President & Chief Executive Officer,
> T. Rowe Price Global Investment Services Limited

"*Customer Tells* provides powerful and practical insights into how customer contact employees can learn to read, and act on the subtle signals that customers often telegraph to employees during an interaction. This is a must-read for leaders at all levels in any organization that deals with customers or consumers directly."

> — Steve Milovich, Senior Vice President Corporate Human Resources,
> The Walt Disney Company

"In the customer service industry, understanding communication styles, how to adapt to the customer, and how to resolve conflict makes your employees well-equipped to deliver excellent customer service while making your whole organization that much stronger. These are the skills in *Customer Tells* that have given our organization an edge in the industry. Not only are these critical pieces of knowledge that can be used in the workplace, but also at home."

> — Leslie White, Vice President, Regional Manager,
> Fremont Investment & Loan

Praise for Dr. Marty Seldman's *Survival of the Savvy*

Wall Street Journal National Bestseller
Fast Company Reader's Choice Award
Harvard Business Review Review of the Month
Institute of Management Studies Book of the Mc

D1025672

"[T]his terrific book shows you don't have to throw your ethics and integrity out of the window to master the game... *Survival of the Savvy* will teach you how to avoid the ego trips and journey to greatness with others."

> — Ken Blanchard, coauthor of the *The One Minute Manager* and
> *Customer Mania*

"*Survival of the Savvy* provides CEOs, business leaders, and their teams with vital new insights and essential skills. The authors set the bar at a new height in describing how to effectively understand and influence others and how to ensure a values-based and high performance work culture."

> — Edward Ludwig, Chairman, CEO, and President, Becton,
> Dickinson and Company

"*Survival of the Savvy* is a critically important book for the new era of business! Leaders need to learn how to win in a world that both ultra-competitive on the business side and ultra-sensitive to issues involving ethics."

— Marshall Goldsmith, coauthor of *The Leaders of the Future*

"A refreshing view of the importance of corporate politics. Survival of the Savvy isn't about the nonsense of stamping our organizational politics—it's about facing reality and learning how to manage yourself and your team, from the CEO down."

— Carol Bartz,Chairman, CEO, AutoDesk

"*Survival of the Savvy* assists CEOs to survey their organizations so that they can build relationship bench strength possessing integrity and ethical management while also building a great company culture committed to top performance and loyalty."

— Ajit Gil, President and Chief Executive Officer, Nektar

"You can influence with political wisdom and integrity! Whether you're a CEO, a teacher, or a new employee, you can continually tune your understanding of yourself and of your work environment. *Survival of the Savvy* is an outstanding tool kit."

— Jim Kennedy, Chief Executive Officer, T. Rowe Price Associates

"This book delivers a powerful message on leadership. Effective leaders learn early that adapting your leadership style to motivate others is one of the most effective skills any leader can possess. *Survival of the Savvy* shows any individual how to step beyond the comfort zone to become a better leader, parent, or person."

— Eric Foss, Chief Executive Officer, Pepsi Bottling Group
North America

"This book has provided me with a systematic understanding of the root cause of company politics and how as a leader once can coach the organization to be mature and effective about managing it. As I have always believed, it takes a politically savvy leader to create an environment that is not excessively political. I just learned a lot from this book on how to become one."

— Sam Su, President, Greater China, YUM Global Restaurants

CUSTOMER TELLS

Delivering World-Class Customer Service by
Reading Your Customers' Signs and Signals

Marty Seldman, PhD
C. John Futterknecht
Benjamin S. Sorensen

PUBLISHING

New York

This publication is designed to provide accurate and authoritative information in regard to the subject matter covered. It is sold with the understanding that the publisher is not engaged in rendering legal, accounting, or other professional service. If legal advice or other expert assistance is required, the services of a competent professional should be sought.

Editorial Editor: Jennifer Farthing
Associate Development Editor: Joshua Martino
Production Editor: Julio Espin
Typesetters: the dotted i, Pamela Beaulieu
Cover Designer: Kathleen Lynch

ISBN-13: 978-1-4195-9609-4
ISBN-10: 1-4195-9609-8

C o n t e n t s

PART THREE

CHANGING CUSTOMER SERVICE CULTURE

As the Vice President of Labor
Relations for MGM MIRAGE, one of the world's leading and most
respected hotel, gaming, and entertainment companies, I am regularly asked to intervene in numerous issues pertaining to the
company's relationship with employees and labor unions. To do
this successfully, active listening, adapting to different personalities, and conflict resolution are some of the critical attributes
needed. Similarly, such skills have never been more needed than
they are now in the area of customer service and guest relations.
In my former role as Vice President of Human Resources for the
MGM Grand Detroit, I saw firsthand the need to build a workforce
that possessed these skills. To accomplish this task, I searched for
tools that would help transform a workforce previously unskilled
in customer service into extraordinary customer service professionals. Unfortunately, I was unsuccessful in finding a tool that
captured the essence of the business's needs. While traveling for
work, however, I unexpectedly found the answer that forever
changed my thinking about customer service.

In May 2005, after a long day at the office, I wasn't looking
forward to a late-night business trip to Chicago. Due to earlier
commitments that day, I had to take the last flight to O'Hare,
which was scheduled to arrive close to or after 11 PM. After a pain-
fully long flight, I hailed a shuttle to whisk me to the hotel. My
thoughts immediately moved to getting my room key and hustling
off to bed. Rest was the first, last, and only thing on my mind.

After arriving at the hotel, I awaited my turn at the registration
desk. It was now close to midnight, and my patience was waning
fast. Through tired eyes, I noticed the guest in front of me carrying
on a very animated discussion with the desk agent, asking about

the best places for nightlife in the area. Their voices were loud, gregarious, and full of excitement—the very behavior I didn't care to encounter that late at night. I feared that I too would receive a similar tone and approach from the desk agent. After the guest in front of me departed, I braced myself for the worst.

To my surprise, the desk agent behaved very differently. She was calm, deliberate, informative, and even tempered. She quickly and professionally checked me in, gave me my room key, and directed me to the hotel elevators.

Amazed by the change, I questioned the desk agent's not-so-subtle transformation. She immediately apologized, thinking that I might have found the change in her attitude offensive. Quite the contrary! In all my years of traveling, this was the first time I had experienced firsthand what I perceived to be the essence of personalized customer service. The agent explained she had noticed that I appeared tired and in need of only minimal direction. Accordingly, she behaved in a way she felt would be most appropriate and effective, given my demeanor at that time. At that moment, it struck me: Customer service is not "one size fits all," but rather a series of unique and very individualized encounters prompted by the customer. Bookstores are filled with literature advocating the need for a uniform method of treating customers. What this experience taught me was the benefit of a more individualized approach.

As an executive in the gaming industry, I immediately recognized that the astute desk agent was reading my *tells*. In card games such as poker, successful players interpret the signals their competitors display. All players except the most expert strategists exhibit some form of *tell* that signals the strength of their hand. Just as in poker, customers will also display tells, signaling how they would most like to be treated. By leveraging customer tells, employees could corner the market in delivering the ultimate level of customer service.

That ten-minute experience forever changed my definition of ultimate customer service. I thought that if other customer service employees could master the same skills as the desk agent in Chicago, the impact on business success could be explosive. The next day, I shared my experience with Dr. Marty Seldman, expert human behaviorist and poker aficionado. I had the pleasure of meeting Dr. Seldman while participating in his executive coaching program. During my session, I learned of Dr. Seldman's success as a competitive poker player earlier in his career. Who better to translate techniques used by skilled poker enthusiasts into tools for managing human behavior? As expected, Dr. Seldman immediately appreciated the value of marrying poker with behavioral tools in order to revolutionize the area of customer service. We explored the possibility of developing a customer service training tool that leveraged the skills I had witnessed the night before. Dr. Seldman, along with his colleagues John Futterknecht and Ben Sorensen, set about designing the framework for the course. Thus began the development of customer tells training. A year later, with the Customer Tells training tool in hand, we set about training frontline employees (those with direct customer contact) at MGM Grand Detroit. Doing so, was no small feat. We were about to pilot the customer tells program at one of the most challenging hospitality environments in our organization. From its opening in 1999, the MGM Grand Detroit had faced significant challenges. A number of employees hired at the new gaming establishment came out of the automotive industry, an environment not known for training and developing customer-focused employees. As a result, the management team at MGM Grand Detroit faced the dilemma of transforming a workforce with a predominantly urban manufacturing mind-set into one suited for the hospitality and service industry. This would be no easy task. After three years of struggles in this area, the management team continued their desperate search for new options, as no training programs seemed to provide the employees with a practical customer service skill set. Because some of the employees had previously undergone more traditional customer service training before taking the customer tells program, they were not looking forward to another class.

To our surprise, the employees readily and enthusiastically embraced the "Customer Tells" philosophy. They instantly recognized the benefits of leveraging the tells customers provided as clues to their preferred treatment. Soon employees became quite adept at reading tells and predicting the most effective customer service response. The training quickly became, and remains, the highest-rated continuous learning course offered. Truly astounding, however, was the reaction of customers. They began flooding the business with letters of approval and appreciation, highlighting the differences they had experienced. Likewise, employees began to look forward to their interactions with guests. Where we once had contentious interchanges between customers and members of the MGM Grand Detroit staff, we now found employees behaving similarly to the astute Chicago desk agent. The effect on business was indeed tremendous: We experienced significant improvement in revenues, market share, and competitive positioning. In short, the training revolutionized our approach to customer service and guest relations. It transformed a workforce that was previously deficient in this critical area into one that leveraged customer tells tools as a competitive advantage.

Employees also recognized the value and usefulness of tells training in all aspects of their lives. They began to use their ability to read tells in their personal lives. They shared numerous stories about using the skills in their interactions and relationships with family, friends, coworkers, and neighbors. They learned to manage their emotions, strengthen their active listening skills, anticipate the needs of others, and defuse tense situations—both professionally and personally—by leveraging tools acquired during the training.

On a personal note, as the parent of a young son, I now routinely use customer tells skills in my relationship with my child. As parents know, predicting a child's behavior is a feat best left to clairvoyants or magicians. While I am neither, I have become more skilled at reading his preteen tells, and modifying my response and approach accordingly. Professionally, I have found customer tells skills to be invaluable in the execution of my professional duties as Vice President of Labor Relations.

In summary, what the Chicago desk agent realized was that people give signals about their preferred treatment all the time. The key is knowing how to give them what they're asking for by listening very carefully to what they say or, more importantly, *what they don't say*. *Customer Tells* will provide the reader with groundbreaking tools to do just that!

Jovita Thomas-Williams
Vice President of Labor Relations
MGM MIRAGE
November 2006

Customers "tell" us how to deliver the highest levels of service. If we pay attention to them, listen to their words, and observe their behavior, they will guide us to do the following:

- Treat them the way they want to be treated.
- Meet and exceed their expectations.
- Provide a positive, predictable experience.
- Develop strong relationships and bonds.
- Tailor our approach to each individual.

THE WORLD OF POKER

Customer Tells is based on a proven training program that has equipped thousands of customer-contact employees with essential skills. The concepts you will learn are drawn from a variety of disciplines, including cognitive psychology, conflict resolution, emotional management, and interpersonal relations.

We have also borrowed from the world of professional poker. *Mike Caro's Book of Tells* (Caro, 2003) defines a *tell* as any behavior, pattern, or reaction a player exhibits that can yield crucial information to an opponent. Poker pros are experts at reading tells, which gives them a great advantage over amateurs. We have found that employees who excel at customer service are also good at reading people. Even more important, we have also discovered that the ability to read people is a learnable skill.

In the world of customer service, we read tells with the goal of satisfying our customers: We want to provide the products, services, and experiences they seek. We consequently define a *customer tell* as any aspect of communication style, body language, behavior, or reaction that reveals a customer's personality, values, needs, and expectations. The customer tell is your key to learning how each specific customer wants to be treated.

There is much more to learn from poker professionals; many of the factors that contribute to their success apply to our customer service goals. In order to win, poker players must:

- Master the fundamentals of the game.
- Manage their emotions.
- Remember people and patterns.
- Read tells.

U.S. presidents, generals, and corporate executives have all attributed part of their success to the lessons they have learned about people while sitting around a poker table. Bobby Baldwin, president and CEO of Mirage Resorts, a division of MGM MIRAGE, is the only person to go from the top of the poker world to the heights of the corporate world. He is a former World Series of Poker champion and the chief executive of a multiproperty division with tens of thousands of employees.

Many of the qualities that made him successful in the poker room, he believes, have helped him make it in the boardroom. He feels his poker experience helped him in the following ways:

- Prepared him for the pure competition of the business world
- Made him comfortable with risk
- Helped him learn to manage his emotions
- Equipped him with the ability to read people and identify personality types
- Taught him that in poker, business, or life, information is king

THE NEED FOR CUSTOMER SERVICE SKILLS

Collectively, corporations spend hundreds of billions of dollars on activities designed to establish their brands. They undertake advertising campaigns, product placement, celebrity endorsements, and a host of other endeavors to create positive impressions of their products and services.

The strategists behind these efforts focus on brand image and positioning, which add up to the ultimate goal of "brand promise." If their product, service, or experience delivers consistently on their brand promise, they will attract many loyal customers who will speak well of the brand. The latest trend is for marketers to try to tailor their brands to changing customer needs.

"Brands are becoming more personalized and customized because consumers want brands on their terms. 'Have it your way' applies increasingly to all brands," says Allen Adamson, managing director of the New York office of Lander Associates, a corporate identity consulting company owned by the WPP Group. However, Mr. Adamson warns, "If you're unable to deliver, if what you offer is really no different from everybody else, the claims will do more damage than good." (Adamson, May 2, 2006)

In most industries, these marketing strategies rely on the customer service employee to deliver the brand promise and customize the product or service to each client's specific needs. It's always somewhat of a gamble when a company establishes its brand's image and then attempts to deliver on that promise. The skill of the employees who interact with customers has a dramatic impact on the success of a brand: Research indicates that the frontline customer service professional often creates the most important perception of the brand. One of our clients in the casino industry recently conducted a survey to determine what differentiated their property from competing casinos in the area. They were happy to find that 65 percent of respondents favored their casino. When they looked at the reasons why, they learned that 61 percent attributed their positive feelings to employees' treatment of them. Specifically these customers mentioned friendliness, politeness, and responsiveness to requests.

Equally interesting is that 36 percent of respondents had low opinions of the casino, and 31 percent of these respondents also attributed their feelings to customer service. Of course, in these cases they wrote about employees who were rude, unresponsive, or inattentive. In many industries, customer service is the true differential between competing companies.

Maria Nalywayko, Senior Vice President of Human Resources at Fremont Investment and Loan, says,

> In the financial services industry, companies tend to compete on price by, for example, offering a better interest rate. Here, while we recognize that price or interest rates are very important to our retail banking customers and our borrowers, we focus first on creating a strong customer value proposition built around an extraordinary customer service experience. In fact, customer service orientation is the first of our five core company values.

We have heard clients within the hotel, restaurant, or casino industries remark that any edge they have from creating a better product or service is temporary. Even if something is working well and connecting with clients, it is only a matter of time until a competitor finds a way to copy it. This is the second reason for building your customer contact employees' skills—it might be the only way to distinguish your company from the competition.

Unfortunately, recent research suggests that many companies are not providing good customer service or delivering brand promise. In August 2006, Discover Financial Services, a division of Morgan Stanley, published the results of a survey of 2,000 adults, assessing their attitudes toward customer service they'd received. They were asked about levels of service in many industries, not just financial services. The survey indicated very high levels of frustration. Keith Heckel, senior vice president for card-member services at Discover, reported,

> As much as companies talk about providing good service, there is a gap between what they say and the reality of what customers experience. This is a call to corporate America that this is an issue that companies need to pay attention to (Lazarus, 2006).

David Lazarus, a business writer for the *San Francisco Chronicle*, writes

> What's interesting here is that consumers are generally saying they want to be treated with respect by any company with which they do business. Yet the level of frustration reflected by the survey suggests that this is precisely what companies aren't doing (Lazarus, 2006). Therefore, the need for excellent customer service is immediate and the impact on the customer is tremendous.

CUSTOMER TELLS OVERVIEW

Here is a road map of what you'll be learning. This book contains three parts.

Part I: The Fundamentals

A poker player can be great at reading tells, but if he or she hasn't mastered the basics of poker—rules, odds, and avoiding "going on tilt," (a poker term meaning letting negative emotions affect your playing)—then he or she will soon be "on the rail," watching the game, but no longer in it. The same principle applies to customer service. If you can read customer tells but don't use basic skills—a positive attitude, respectful behavior, good listening, emotional management, conflict resolution, and win-win problem-solving tools—you won't help yourself or your company. That's why Part I focuses on the Golden Rule: Treat people the way you want to be treated. You will learn about the fundamental behaviors all customers expect, and how to develop and demonstrate them consistently. Additionally, you will learn how these fundamentals are the building blocks for the customer tells skills of Part II.

Part I includes:

• Self-talk
• Listening skills
• Problem solving
• Dealing with the on-tilt customer

Part II: Customer Tells

In this section of the book, you will go beyond the Golden Rule, and apply the Platinum Rule, named by Robert and Dorothy Bolton, which is: Treat people the way *they* want to be treated (Alessandra, O'Connor, 1996). After you have mastered the basics—listening, respect, and responsiveness—you can't just fall back on a one-size-fits-all approach. You will learn that if you pay attention, there is a rich flow of information your customers are sending your way. If you can learn to recognize the distinctive characteristics of each customer, you can then tailor your approach so you meet or exceed his or her expectations.

Daniel Goleman, in his best-selling book *Social Intelligence* (2006), provides an excellent illustration of this blend of awareness and adaptability:

At a local restaurant there's a waitress everyone loves to have serve them. She has an uncanny knack for matching the mood and pace of her customers, gliding into synch.

She's quiet and discreet with the morose man nursing a drink at that table over there in the dark corner. But then she's sociable and outgoing with a noisy batch of coworkers laughing it up on their lunch hour. And for that young mom with two hyperactive toddlers, she wades right into the frenzy, entrancing the kids with some funny faces and jokes. Understandably, this waitress gets by far the biggest tips of any.

In Part II you will learn about several levels of customer tells:

- In-the-moment tells
- Customer communication style tells
- Cultural tells
- Third-party tells

Part III: Changing Customer Service Culture

As trainers, we understand the importance of reinforcing and supporting new learning in a customer service environment. In this section we share our experiences with companies that have worked to make the skills and attitudes of customer tells part of their culture. You will learn about the roles of supervisors, managers, and senior executives in modeling and reinforcing these skills. We also show you how customer service skills can become part of your hiring processes.

Finally, we hope to show you that your frontline employees are potentially your best market researchers. With the right systems for capturing information, customer tells skills can translate into timely customer insights.

Customer Tells Skills

Each skill you learn in *Customer Tells* meets our criteria for being a *core*, *multiuse*, and *life* skill.

Core skills. We are strong believers in mastering the basics. Essential skills might seem like second nature, but remember the adage: Common sense is not always common practice. If you consistently demonstrate core skills, you will be more effective in most endeavors.

Multiuse skills. We love multiuse skills. Not only do you reap multiple benefits from mastering them, but you can also find a lot of opportunities to practice them. Participants in our customer tells seminars told us that these skills helped them to get along better with coworkers, friends, and family.

Life skills. Customer tells skills will not become obsolete; they are straightforward, practical, and easy to adapt to different situations. We wish each of you a long, healthy life, and are confident you will be using these skills for a long time.

Part One

THE FUNDAMENTALS

1

THE GOLDEN RULE
*Treat Others the Way
You Want to Be Treated*

In the introduction we discussed the impact of high-quality customer service on a company's overall success. What impact does it have on you, the frontline customer service professional? The answer is simple: As the individual who touches the customer first, you hold one of the most critical roles in the company!

To prove this point, you need look no further than your own experience. Have you ever called or visited a business that attracted you with a clever commercial, or with a product that had a stellar reputation? Yet, within five minutes of interacting with a customer service professional (and sometimes it takes far less time), you began figuring out the quickest way to leave the store or end the call.

Alternatively, you have also likely experienced the pleasure of receiving outstanding customer service. The kind of interaction that left you thinking, "Now that is what customer service should be. I am going to buy from this company every chance I get."

The key question to ask ourselves as customer service professionals is: What are the essential behaviors that will consistently provide for excellent customer service interaction and what are the behaviors that will likely lead to bad customer service? The answer to this question is what Part I, the Golden Rule Fundamentals, is all about. Fortunately, the answer is no great mystery. We are all customers ourselves and, therefore, our own experience informs us what makes up good customer service. This is why we refer to the skills that will consistently provide outstanding customer service as the *Golden Rule* Fundamentals—it is about treating the customer the way we want to be treated.

As your personal experience will probably confirm, research shows that there are three core behaviors that every customer wants customer service professionals to display: positive attitude, listening, and being responsive to the customer's needs.

Positive Attitude

One of the most important aspects of a customer service interaction is an employee's positive attitude. This sets the tone for the whole exchange. If a customer is met by an employee exuding enthusiasm and a clear desire to help, the encounter is off to an excellent start. John experiences the power of positive attitude when he visits his local bank. One particular bank teller named Winnie has such positive energy that it is literally contagious. On several occasions John has entered the bank in a state of negativity and within the first 20 seconds of interacting with Winnie he is in a better mood. Her warm smile, kind tone of voice, and clear enthusiasm for her work help John feel positive, extremely valued, and confident that his needs will be met.

Conversely, it is possible to ruin a customer service interaction without saying a word. Think about the saying, "A picture is worth a thousand words." If your body language, facial expression, and tone of voice are communicating your reluctance to talk with a customer, the interaction is likely doomed before it has begun. Even if you say the right words, if your body language is communicating something different, studies show that a person will respond to the body language. Ben recently had such an experience at a local dry cleaner. He visited the business to drop off some clothes he needed for work the next week. As he entered the shop he noticed two employees behind the counter engaged in a conversation. After waiting a few moments Ben asked, "Excuse me, I wanted to drop off these clothes please." The employee nearest to him turned and rolled her eyes. Her annoyed facial expression seemed to say, "Can't you see that I was in the middle of a conversation?" Despite this annoyed look she said, "how may I help you?" Although she may have said the right words, her body language said, "you are a huge aggravation so can we get this over with so I can get back to my conversation?" Needless to say, Ben found another dry cleaner. Remember the first core behavior, a positive attitude if crucial to your success as a customer service professional.

Listening

Another universal expectation of the customer is that the customer service professional listen to them. Being listened to fulfills several important needs for the customer. First and foremost, excellent listening (in combination with a positive attitude) is perhaps the most powerful way to demonstrate respect. Since being treated respectfully is of the highest priority for virtually all customers, skillful listening is critical. Skillful listening builds trust and rapport, two key elements towards our objectives of building relationships and loyalty. Additionally, customers expect to be listened to so that they have an opportunity to explain what their needs are and, if they have a concern or complaint, they also expect to be heard. Overall, great listening can have an extremely positive impact on a customer service interaction.

Just as effective listening can win customers for life, poor listening has the potential to create frustration, mistrust and missing the customer's top priority. Even the *impression* of not being listened to while speaking can almost immediately leave a customer feeling as though they are not being treated with respect. Furthermore, an aggravation like being led to a product in a store that is not what you asked for will usually set the wrong tone. Finally, not having the opportunity to discuss your frustration when something went wrong can only make matters worse. Therefore, to perform well as a customer service professional we must excel in listening.

Responsive to Needs

In addition to a positive attitude and skillful listening, the third core expectation of all customers is a sense that we are responsive to their needs. Broadly speaking, *responsive to their needs* is about the customer having an experience which leaves them feeling important, treated fairly, well attended to, and that all was done on behalf of the customer service professional to meet their needs. This experience is achieved in a number of ways including: attending to the customer with minimal wait time, demonstrating a genuine interest in the customer's needs and priorities, and, in the case of a disagreement, communicating with the customer such that they feel they were respected and that all options were explored to get them what they wanted. Ben recently had the pleasure of such an experience while taking his car in for servicing at the car dealership.

The purpose for Ben's visit was a malfunction in the car's acceleration, which had him quite frustrated as the car was not too old. Almost immediately upon arrival at the dealership Ben was greeted by a professional who gave Ben his full attention to hear about the problem. After apologizing for the inconvenience, the mechanic quickly examined the car and discovered that a wire involved in the acceleration process had been damaged. Although this particular wire was not covered under the car's general warranty, the dealership found a way to defray most of the cost. In addition, while Ben was there he also asked for an oil change only for the dealership to explain that his car was not due for another one thousand miles. Even though Ben started the day frustrated with the car company, he left the dealership happy, with a greater sense of loyalty, and he decided that from that day forth he would bring his car to the dealership for all issues including basic maintenance even though it was more expensive than some other options.

If a customer feels as though their needs were not responded to in the ways described above they are more likely to be an unsatisfied and one-time customer. Often, the mere appearance that a customer service professional is lacking the effort to minimize the customer's wait time is enough to upset and turn off the customer. Similarly, the feeling that a customer service professional is trying to convince you to make a decision because it is in their best interest (e.g., a larger commission, more profit for the company, less effort on their part) as opposed to the customer's best interest will quickly create mistrust. Finally, if you have ever been in a situation where you feel you had been wronged by a company and then during your efforts to correct the situation you were treated in a way that felt disrespectful and unfair you know how strong that negative reaction can be.

John recently experienced a combination of customer service mistakes with his former cell phone company. John had called his cell phone company to increase the number of minutes on his plan because he was going on a long trip and knew he would be spending more time on his cell phone than usual. It was his understanding that the increase in minutes was effective immediately after his call. However, he was very unpleasantly surprised when he opened his next phone bill to discover that the increase in minutes had not been activated until the next billing cycle and, therefore, he was charged a high rate for several hundred minutes. When John called to inquire about the issue he initially waited over 20 minutes for the first operator to pick up and then was transferred to four different individuals before he had the appropriate person on the other line. Then after the long wait, he was told, "I can't help you Sir; that is company policy." To make matters worse, even after John had explained that the particular month was an exception and that he rarely used that many minutes, the individual proceeded to try and convince him to further upgrade his current plan to one which had almost twice as many minutes as he ordinarily used because it would include unused minutes "which would accumulate over time and eliminate this from happening in the future"—hardly John's concern. After hearing that story, you are probably not surprised to hear that this is John's "former" cell phone company.

Once we are aware of the key components all customers are looking for in a satisfactory experience our goal is to exhibit these behaviors skillfully and consistently.

There is something at stake in each and every interaction. One bad customer service experience is often enough to cause the customer to turn to a different store or brand. Furthermore, we also tend to tell friends and family about our bad experience. In fact, on average a person who has a bad customer service incident will tell ten people about it. Not only does the word spread about the bad experience—which hurts the company—but it also resembles the telephone game we played as children: Passing a message from one person to another often changes the story, at times making it worse. The company will not just lose one customer, it may also lose many others without even being aware of it.

The good news is that providing excellent customer service is not only great in the short term; it has great long-tem pay off as well. Why? People like to have a predictable customer service experience. There are likely several different restaurants and fast food establishments where you live, but don't you find yourself going to one more than the others? Often we like to stick with what works and where we know what we are going to get. In one city Marty often visits, there are three hotels in close proximity to each other. Each offers basically the same services. Does Marty rotate with which hotel he stays? No—he always stays in the one where he feel most comfortable. This means that if you provide excellent customer service once, you will reap the benefits in the future.

So, how can we ensure consistent success with the customer? The Golden Rule Fundamentals.

The Golden Rule Fundamentals

The Golden Rule Fundamentals are a collection of skills that, if practiced, will ensure that you will always meet the customer's essential needs. It is our aim to provide you these core skills with great depth and practicality. We chose the term fundamentals to convey their importance. And, just as any coach might, we will encourage you to continuously strive to improve in all of these areas. In the world of athletics the value of fundamentals is well understood. When basketball coach Pat Riley led the Los Angeles Lakers to several championships in the 1980s he always stressed the importance of fundamentals. In fact, his main strategy for winning each year was not an elaborate or complicated scheme, it was challenging all of his players to improve in the fundamental areas of their game such as defense, free throw shooting, and shooting percentage. Similarly, the best customer service professionals realize that the fundamentals are crucial, can always be improved, and serve as the foundation of everything they do.

The potential risk when discussing fundamentals, which will often be referred to as the basics, is that they may be taken for granted and, therefore, not given sufficient focus in regards to growth and development. Do not make this mistake. Fundamentals are simple but not easy. As you learn the Golden Rule Fundamentals, reflect on your current level of expertise, get feedback from others as to how well you perform in each area, and challenge yourself to improve.

2

SELF-TALK
Creating a Positive Attitude

*There is a person with whom you spend more time with than any other, a person
who has more influence over your growth than anyone else. This ever-present
companion is your own self. This self guides you, belittles you, or supports you.*

*You engage this person in an ever-constant dialogue—a dialogue through which
you set goals for yourself, make decisions, feel pleased, dejected, or despondent.
In short, your behavior, feelings, sense of self-esteem, and even level of stress
are influenced by your inner speech.*

—Pamela Butler, *Talking to Yourself*, (1991)

The first fundamental aspect of de-
livering excellent customer service is the creation and maintenance
of a positive attitude. Controlling your attitude, or emotional management, is central to a poker player's success and vital to working
successfully with customers. The poker professional needs mental
discipline and toughness in order to maintain concentration, stay
focused, and remain positive. Poker is a game of patience as good
and bad hands often come in streaks. As a result, it is essential to
keep a confident frame of mind even after a *bad beat,* a hand in
which one player strategically outplayed another but the opponent
draws a lucky card to win. A negative attitude after a bad hand can
affect the player's perception of risk, level of confidence, and the
behavioral cues or tells that he or she displays to opponents.

For you, the customer service professional, the cost of a negative attitude is greater. While the poker player might get a chance

to recover any losses, you probably will not. As Will Rogers once remarked, "You never get a second chance to make a first impression." This is particularly true for the customer service professional: A negative attitude and its resulting behavior can, within seconds, negatively shape the entire customer interaction. Therefore, what happens between your ears, your emotional management, is critical to your success as a customer service professional.

Customer service is an emotional business. Research in customer service and sales have shown that certain emotions on the part of a professional lead to positive levels of customer service and sales and certain negative emotions hurt customer service and sales. See Figure 2.1. Therefore, it is imperative that customer service professionals rely on their ability to maximize time spent utilizing valuable emotions while consciously working to minimize less desirable emotions.

Capturing and maintaining our positive emotions is critical. Therefore we need more reliable ways to generate positive emotions than just hoping we wake up in a good mood every morning. As a customer service professional, it is essential to determine, practice, and master ways to create positive emotions. The key to gaining greater awareness of our emotions is understanding that they are predominately generated through our *self-talk*.

FIGURE 2.1 *Range of Customer Service Emotions*

MOST VALUABLE EMOTIONS

- Friendliness and liking people
- Enthusiasm about your product
- High energy level
- Enjoying what you do
- Confidence
- Wanting to help people
- Relaxed alertness
- Gratitude and appreciation

LEAST VALUABLE EMOTIONS

- Unfriendliness and irritability
- Frustration and anger
- "Down" feelings, low energy
- Pessimism about your product
- Worry and anxiety
- Feeling of not being in control
- Distracted

WHAT IS SELF-TALK?

Our thoughts lead to feelings and feelings lead to behaviors. Thoughts are essentially the dialogue going on in our head. In case you were concerned about the fact that you talk to yourself —you can stop worrying, it is natural—everyone does it! Furthermore, this conversation in our head is going on all the time. It is this inner dialogue that we call self-talk. Not only is our self-talk occurring continuously, it happens at a feverish pace. While we speak at a rate of about 150 words a minute, psychologists estimate that we talk to ourselves at a rate of *600 to 800* words a minute! This *self-talk* has a profound impact on our feelings. Our emotions, moods, and attitudes don't simply happen to us. The trouble is we rarely think about what we think about—now think about that! In the next section we more closely examine self-talk and its power—both negative and positive—on our behavior.

THE POWER OF SELF-TALK

Self-talk is our internal reaction and response to events that happen to us. Allow us to give an example of the power of self-talk. Say it's Friday evening and you and a friend have been invited to a party. The two of you walk into the party and begin talking with a group of people whom you are meeting for the first time. At one point, a woman says something rude to your friend about his attitude. You keep talking with the group but you notice that your friend is now quiet and sulking. The rest of the time at the party he seems uncharacteristically reserved and stands by himself for parts of the night. As you are leaving the party you ask him if he had a good time and he responds, "That woman ruined my entire night."

Did she ruin his night? Who really ruined his night? Arguably, he ruined his own night. She may have been rude to him, but he also responded to the situation in a particular way. What was his likely self-talk? Possibly, "Why doesn't she like me? What is wrong with me? I'm always so bad at meeting new people." How did this self-talk affect his feelings? It likely led to feelings of sadness, frustration, loneliness, and self-pity. These feelings consequently created a mood and perception of looking unhappy. We term this type of self-talk *unhelpful* self-talk because it can lead to feelings that can be very unhelpful and self-defeating. This example illustrates how unhelpful self-talk leads to counterproductive emotions and behavior.

What if instead of blaming the woman for spoiling his night, your friend's self-talk was "That's just one person's opinion," "Who is she? She doesn't even know me," or "Maybe she had a bad day and hasn't gotten over it yet"? If this is what he was thinking, is he likely to have a better time at the party? Of course. This is one example of positive self-talk—self-talk that helps create emotions which leads to improved productivity, a positive attitude and greater enjoyment of a situation.

Let's apply self-talk to the customer service profession. If a customer service professional engages in unhelpful self-talk, for example, thinking to herself, "why do I always have to answer this same question over and over again?" she is likely to feel a little annoyed or somewhat frustrated. Feeling this way, is she likely to go above and beyond for the customer? Is she likely to have a positive attitude? Feeling this way, it is very unlikely, if not impossible, to have a positive attitude and is very challenging to deliver excellent customer service. Alternatively, saying, "answering questions is part of what I do and is always an opportunity to create a satisfied customer" is much more likely to help the customer service professional feel enthusiastic, friendly, and confident. Creating these positive emotions helps us as customer service professionals to deliver excellent service while feeling generally good about ourselves and what we are doing.

As the quote at the start of the chapter points out, your self-communications can create both positive and negative results. You are likely to talk to yourself before, during, and after customer contacts—sometimes helping and sometimes hurting your chances for success. Just as the poker player uses mental discipline and toughness to maintain concentration and remain positive, customer service professionals must motivate themselves to choose their words carefully, display the right body language, and speak in an appropriate tone of voice. We have tracked thousands of customer service interactions and have found that when patrons complain of poor customer service, often the customer service professional who served that person had thoughts that were negative in nature.

When we are engaged in unhelpful self-talk it affects not only how we feel, but how we feel is reflected in our body language. Think back to your friend at the party, his body language clearly reflected his unhelpful self-talk. With approximately 85 percent of our communication delivered through body language, our non-verbal cues are a very powerful mode of interacting with our customers. Customers can sense our agitation or frustration very quickly from our body language, which can compromise an entire interaction. Our body language is very difficult to mask, so it's all the more important to turn unhelpful self-talk positive to ensure a productive customer interaction.

Self-talk skills not only benefit customer service professionals, salespeople, and poker players; they are often utilized to enhance the performance of top athletes and artists. For example, athletes who regularly use positive self-talk enhance performance by managing their emotions and creating a positive expectation for a situation. Golfer Tiger Woods uses self-talk to help determine how he wants to hit a shot before swinging, and he credits his self-talk with helping him achieve greater success on the golf course. The frequency, duration, and intensity of unwanted stressful emotions can all be reduced with positive self-talk, and improvement in each of these dimensions allows you to have more effective customer service interactions.

For a moment, think about the best coach, teacher, or counselor you've ever known. Think of someone who knew just what to say to guide, encourage, and motivate you, or to help you bounce back from disappointments. With the skills and strategies of this chapter, you can develop your own inner coach, who will take *positive control* of your self-talk and emotions. This coach knows your good habits and your bad ones, your strengths and the areas in which you need to improve, and the attitudes and emotions that help you perform and those that block your forward progress. Your inner counselor will mentally prepare you for your best possible customer service interactions; reduce fear, anger, and discouragement; deal with pressure; get you back on track; and help you improve. You will develop the ability to perform consistently during adverse conditions—and, finally, you will learn to enjoy what you do.

Now that we have a clear picture of the impact self-talk has on our success we will shift our attention to a more in-depth understanding of the nature of self-talk and the core skills for success.

SELF-TALK IS A HABIT

Before we transition to the skills portion of the chapter, there are a few aspects of self-talk that are useful to understand. First, our self-talk is primarily habitual. The nature and power of habits are a common thread throughout the book and we discuss them in great detail in Chapter 10. For now, let us say that our self-talk— or what we say to ourselves—is primarily an automatic response that has been ingrained over time. From our perspective this is a positive because it means that as we become aware of our self-talk, we can anticipate the kinds of experiences that are likely to trigger unhelpful self-talk and, even better, with practice we can eventually change current unhelpful self-talk habits and create positive ones.

Helpful Self-talk Is Realistic and Useful—
It Is Not "Positive Thinking"

Our approach to mastering our self-talk is not what is commonly known as *positive thinking*. An example of positive thinking would be to suggest that when your natural reaction to a customer is, "this guy is my worst nightmare! If it weren't for customers like this I would actually enjoy my job," you force the self-talk of, "Yes! I am so happy he is here—this is going to make my day!" In our experience, choosing self-talk which is in-authentic and doesn't feel true is not that effective in the long term. We do however recommend realistic and useful self-talk. The distinction is that the self-talk phrase you choose is both true and helpful in creating a more positive emotional state. For instance, going back to the previous example, one possibility of realistic and useful self-talk would be, "This customer is a challenge for me, but I am a professional with the skills to deliver excellent service even under these circumstances." Later in the chapter we will discuss the process of choosing positive self-talk in great detail. Here we just want to clarify that you are entitled to think and feel whatever is true for you. It is not a matter of labeling thoughts and feelings as good or bad, rather, our focus is on which thoughts and feelings are more and less valuable in performing well in your role as a customer service professional or salesperson. As a result, our focus will be on the insight and skills necessary to increase your valuable emotions.

The recognition that our self-talk is mostly habitual and our focus on realistic and useful self-talk shape our overall approach. For the remainder of the chapter we will focus on the core skills and strategies of effectively mastering your self-talk.

MASTERING YOUR SELF-TALK

Step 1. Know Thy Self-Talk

The media theorist Marshall McLuhan (1969) said, "I don't know who discovered water, but it wasn't a fish." By this he meant that fish cannot see the water that surrounds them, and likewise, we often can't perceive our own mental patterns because they are so much a part of us. Remember our phrase from earlier— we rarely think about what we think about. We have all tried to change habits we are aware of and we know firsthand how difficult that can be. If that is hard, how hard is it to change habits we may not consciously even know we have? It's practically impossible. This is why the first step to improving your self-talk skills is increasing your awareness.

You can experiment right now—how are you reacting to these words? Are you agreeing or disagreeing? What's your self-talk? As a practice, begin to pay attention to your inner dialogue more regularly as you are working. In particular, consciously listen to your self-talk anytime you find yourself in a less valuable emotional state (i.e. angry, irritable, or anxious). Remember, your thoughts create and sustain your emotions so if you are feeling one of these emotions such as anger there is almost surely a conversation happening from within that is reinforcing it. Additionally, since you know that your self-talk is habitual, you are likely to notice that there are similarities between particular experiences and people (a customer, a co-worker, or a supervisor) and unhelpful self-talk. As a result, the more you study your self-talk and learn these patterns, the more you will able to anticipate who and what is likely to trigger the unhelpful inner chatter. It is also useful to take note of your self-talk when you are feeling more helpful emotions (i.e. enthusiasm, confidence, or friendliness) because these emotions, naturally, are also accompanied by corresponding self-talk. By learning what type of inner dialogue tends to create more valuable emotions, you can choose to use those phrases in place of unhelpful ones. This can be a very powerful practice because you know they are phrases that work for you.

Step 2. The Power of Choice

Hopefully you recognize that you play a very instrumental role in your ongoing self-talk. Our self-talk is our internal reaction and response to events that happen to us. We all can, at times, feel prisoner to our self-talk. These experiences create a sense that our self-talk is out of our control and is just a result of how we react to situations. However, just as when we choose to respond to an accusation by verbally defending ourselves or jumping up and down when our favorite sports team scores, with insight and practice, we have the ability to choose our self-talk. While we definitely cannot control the behavior of others or events that occur, we can control the self-talk we focus on. In fact, in any situation, you have the power to choose what you focus on and what you say to yourself. We are not happy, concerned or frustrated because of an event but we feel this way because of how we *react* to an event. More accurately, we feel this way because of how our self-talk responds to an event.

Once you have gained awareness of your unhelpful self-talk phrases and patterns, the next crucial step is learning to consciously choose effective, positive self-talk that creates the more valuable emotional state you want. To learn this skill, let's begin by examining a real-life example of a customer service professional interacting with a guest:

Jill works at a major hotel chain in a large city and deals with business travelers regularly. They are generally pleasant to her but they are also usually in a hurry. One evening Jill is working at the front desk when a business traveler rushes up to her.

Traveler, throwing her credit card at Jill: "I am checking in."

Jill: "Okay. Welcome to the hotel. One minute while I pull up your reservation." Checking the computer, Jill discovers that the traveler doesn't have a reservation.

Jill: "I'm sorry, ma'am, but there is no reservation under your name."

Traveler: "What are you talking about? I don't have time for this. I made the reservation months ago. Why don't you get me someone who can actually help me?"

Jill turns to go into the back to get a manager.

What would your self-talk be if you were Jill? How is Jill's self-talk going to affect her interaction with this customer, and possibly her next customer as well? Let's assume that her self-talk goes like this: "Great. I know this is going to be one of those shifts where nothing goes right. I should just go home instead of dealing with this."

How will Jill's self-talk influence her experience with the traveler? She is likely to be thoroughly annoyed and might hold on to that attitude for a good part of the evening, which will, in turn, likely to effect how she interacts with other customers.

UNHELPFUL SELF-TALK

Although we can agree that Jill's self talk is less than ideal, we certainly would not label her as an unreasonable or bad person. It is completely normal to face challenging situations with customers that can result in similar forms of unhelpful self-talk. Just as Jill may have initially had some unhelpful talk, it is not unusual for real-world customer service professionals to use some of the following self-talk phrases. As you read the self-talk below, try to imagine how this person is feeling. Get a mental picture of what their verbal and nonverbal behavior might be. Also, take note of any phrases that you recognize as phrases you use on occasion.

- If they would just read the sign, they'd know what to do and wouldn't keep bothering me.
- I know this is going to be one of those days where nothing goes right.

- I don't know what those geniuses in marketing are thinking. I've had to spend the whole day explaining things to people.
- I guess some people don't care what they look like when they go out in public.
- It's not my fault that he's upset with the products or services we offer. I don't want to deal with people who have such bad attitudes.
- My break starts in five minutes. Just my luck that I have two clueless guests walk up to me now!
- I have more important things going on in my life than what's happening here at work.
- This is typical. I can spot these people a mile away. They think they are better than everyone else.

Even though this self-talk is normal and in fact common, it isn't helpful. Hopefully you would agree that each of the phrases—if focused on—would likely generate a less valuable emotion. As most of us will have unhelpful self-talk some of the time the key is our ability to quickly shift our focus and replace it with the positive.

REPLACING UNHELPFUL SELF-TALK

Great athletes, poker players, and great customer service professionals have all learned how to quickly identify and replace their unhelpful self-talk. We'll teach you our method by applying it to the list of unhelpful self-talk phrases above. The process is a combination of mental strategies for shifting your focus and choosing positive self-talk phrases for replacement.

If they would just read the sign, they'd know what to do and they wouldn't keep bothering me. Changing this negative opinion into a positive attitude can be as simple as putting yourself in your customer's shoes—if you refuse to consider your customer's side of things, your bad attitude may backfire on you. One professional became annoyed with guests always asking where the bathroom was. There were plenty of signs pointing the way. Finally, toward the end of the day, yet another guest asked him where the bathroom was. The frustrated employee snapped, "Follow the signs. Can't you read?" The guest replied, "No, actually, I can't."

By letting his frustration get the best of him, the employee likely lost a customer for life.

Always try to see the customer's point of view. There many reasons why a guest might not be able to read a sign: perhaps she is elderly and her sight is failing, or maybe English is not her first language. Maybe it is her first time in the hotel and she isn't quite sure where to look. Try to empathize with her. Have you ever been in the grocery store and asked a clerk where a certain item was, only to be shown that it was right in front of you? It's easy to miss signs.

If you use unhelpful self-talk when a customer misses a sign, your body language and tone of voice will reflect your mood. You likely will look tense and sound irritated. Be aware that you are talking to yourself in a nonproductive manner, and choose to change this self-talk into positive statements such as:

- If people didn't get confused or didn't have questions, my place of business wouldn't need me.
- I have the skills to help this guest and deal with this situation.
- I like to help people solve their problems.

I know this is going to be one of those days where nothing goes right. This statement is commonly triggered by something going wrong early in the day. You burned breakfast, forgot the dry cleaning, spilled something, or are having a bad hair day. It can become what is called a *self-fulfilling prophecy*. The sociologist Robert Merton coined the term self-fulfilling prophecy and defined it as a false definition of a situation evoking a new behavior that makes the originally false perception come true. If you stay focused on this unhelpful self-talk, it may actually come true. Why? This self-talk tends to lead to reduced motivation and effort, a tendency to give up after mistakes. As a result, there is a far greater likelihood events will in fact "not go right," supporting your initial statement with a resounding: "See, I knew it." I suppose the one benefit of this way of thinking it does allow you be right!

Alternatively, positive self-talk gives you confidence, helps you overcome setbacks, and allows you to make progress toward a positive result. By choosing positive self-talk phrase you are likely to create a positive self-fulfilling prophesy. More positive self-talk options are:

- This mistake may be a sign that I'm rushing things or didn't do enough planning. I will slow down before I create more problems.
- This is an inconvenience, but it's only one thing wrong. I can make the rest of the day positive and productive.
- Everybody has a bad hair day sometimes. I can laugh at myself, have some fun with it, and create a relaxed atmosphere for the people I interact with today.

Any of these self-talk statements is more helpful than "I know this will be one of those days where nothing goes right."

I don't know what those geniuses in marketing are thinking. I've got to spend the whole day explaining things to people. Your company's marketing team may well be flawed, but that's not the guests' fault. Perhaps you can talk to the marketing department later on and air your concerns. For now, don't let your frustration affect your customer interactions. Positive self-talk in this situation can include:

- I'll give feedback to marketing so that it can make things more clear. At least these programs are bringing people in the door.
- This is an opportunity to really be helpful to a guest.

I guess some people don't care what they look like when they go out in public. Be careful not to judge your customer. One participant in a seminar once remarked that she would dress more casually the costlier the purchase she made. Her intention was that when she would make a large purchase, such as a car, the salesperson who did not judge her buying power based on her clothing would receive the commission. Therefore, focus on the positive:

- I'm glad this guest feels so comfortable in our establishment.

It's not my fault that he's upset with the products or services we offer. I don't want to deal with people who have such bad attitudes. If you listen to this unhelpful self-talk your body language becomes defensive and your customer can quickly assume you don't care about their problem or that you are refusing to take responsibility for the problem. If you allow the customer's attitude to affect yours, your bad mood could then rub off on other customers and coworkers. Instead of putting up your defenses when an upset guest approaches, you could tell yourself:

- I will not take this personally. He's probably upset with something that I had nothing to do with, but I can use my abilities to try to meet his needs.
- I can never control other people, but I can influence them by using my skills. If I want to influence their decisions and actions most effectively, I need to listen to them, understand them, and see things from their perspective.

My break starts in five minutes. Just my luck that I have two clueless guests walk up to me now. These guests had a choice. They could have gone somewhere else. If your attitude indicates that you are irritated by their questions or that you are anxious to go on your break, the guests may well go somewhere else next time. By helping them and staying positive, you show them that they made the right choice by coming to your place of work. Some positive self-talk that you can use includes:

- These guests had a choice today. They could have gone to a competitor. I'm going to show them that they made the right decision.
- Problems or questions give me an opportunity to use my skills and develop deeper bonds with a guest.

I have more important things going on in my life than what's happening here at work. This is true for many of us. It doesn't mean, however, that work is unimportant. After all, work pays for all those important things going on in your life. You can change this negative attitude into a positive one by telling yourself:

- I have other things going on in my life, but I can't do anything about them while I'm at work. The best thing I can do for myself and for the company is to focus on the guest in front of me.
- This guest is helping me pay my bills and support my family.

This is typical. I can spot these people a mile away. They think they are better than everyone else. Notice how this kind of self-talk will likely lead to a defensive and even aggressive posture which is the opposite of the kinds of emotions you want to create. When you feel confident you are much more optimistic about your ability to satisfy a difficult customer. One customer service professional told us that she could spot troublesome guests from across the room. When she sees one approaching, she mentally prepares herself to be as friendly as she possibly can. "Kill them with kindness," she says. When the guest responds well to her pleasant manner, she thinks to herself, "Well, I won that round." If you come across a customer whose attitude you can't change, don't let that customer change your positive attitude. Don't let grumpy clients take you out of your game use these self-talk alternatives:

- I have the skills to help this guest and deal with this situation.
- No one can push my buttons but me. I choose how I react people and situations.
- I will not let the unpleasant experience with this guest affect how I treat other guests.

These are a few examples of how to choose positive self-talk to increase our ultimate goal: maximize the time we spend in more valuable emotions and minimize the time we spend in the less valuable. As an additional reference, we provided you with a chart that lists examples of unhelpful self-talk on the left and positive self-talk to replace it on the right.

Unhelpful Self-Talk	Positive Self-Talk Replacement
If they would just read the sign, they'd know what to do and wouldn't keep bothering me.	If people didn't get confused or didn't have questions, my place of business wouldn't need me.
I know this is going to be one of those days where nothing goes right.	This is an inconvenience, but it's only one thing wrong. I can make the rest of the day positive and productive.
I don't know what those geniuses in marketing are thinking. I've had to spend the whole day explaining things to people.	I'll give feedback to marketing so that they can make things more clear. At least these programs are bringing people in the door.

Unhelpful Self-Talk	Positive Self-Talk Replacement
I guess some people don't care what they look like when they go out in public.	I'm glad this guest feels so comfortable in our establishment.
It's not my fault that he's upset with the products or services we offer. I don't want to deal with people who have such bad attitudes.	I'm not going to take this personally. He's probably upset with something that I had nothing to do with, but I can use my abilities to try to meet his needs.
My break starts in five minutes. Just my luck that I have two clueless guests walk up to me now!	These guests had a choice today. They could have gone to a competitor. I will show them that they made the right decision.
I have more important things going on in my life than what's happening here at work.	Work is not unimportant. Work helps pay for all the things going in my life, and helps me provide for myself and for my family.
This is typical. I can spot these people a mile away. They think they are better than everyone else.	I have the skills to help this guest and deal with this situation. No one can push my buttons but me.

In Figure 2.2, below, write down some of the unhelpful self-talk you use and try some of the strategies from the examples to shift your focus and choose a positive self-talk phrase to replace it. We realize that effective positive self-talk can very personal and specific to the individual and while we have offered you many examples as a tool to help you, feel free to customize them or come up with your own. Remember that capturing your self-talk during more valuable emotional states is a great resource.

Investing time in improving your self-talk has both short and long term benefits. In the short term, effectively using the skills described will help generate the positive emotions you want while interacting with a guest, laying the foundation of an excellent interaction. Also, if you practice the skill consistently, in time your old unhelpful self-talk habit will be completely replaced by the new positive self-talk which is now an automatic response!

FIGURE 2.2 *Replacing My Unhelpful Self-Talk*

UNHELPFUL SELF-TALK	POSITIVE SELF-TALK REPLACEMENT

STARTING POSITIVE
"A Check Up from the Neck Up"

One of the best ways you can create positive attitudes and emotions in yourself is to start your day with positive self-talk. The motivational speaker Zig Zigler calls this "A Check Up from the Neck Up," and it's an excellent way to start your day off in the right emotional state. You might say it is proactive positive self-talk. If you are already in a positive emotional state, you are less likely to move into or remain stuck in unhelpful self-talk. Here are some positive self-talk phrases that work:

- I like to meet people and I focus on their good qualities.
- My goal is to make each person glad he talked with me.
- The guests help me pay my bills and support my family.
- Every day I am learning more about our customers, and that will help me meet their expectations.
- I have the skills to perform my job with excellence.
- I like to help people solve their problems.
- I can create positive results in any situation.
- No one else can dictate how I feel today.
- Problems give me an opportunity to use my skills and develop deeper bonds with a guest.

Choose one or more of the phrases above or feel free to create your own that resonate with you more strongly. Make it a habit to perform your "Check Up from the Neck Up," while driving into work, as you begin your shift, on breaks, or any other time you need a boost.

You are now equipped with the core skills and awareness to take positive control of your self-talk. As with most skills, the way to fully realize the benefits is dedicated practice. As you move forward in improving your skills, we would like to warn you of the damaging effects of spending too much time with perpetually negative coworkers. We have heard many stories of that coworker who is always unhappy, who believes the customers sole purpose in life is to make your life difficult, who generally the see the cup as always half-empty, and otherwise seem to chose complaining as a religion! The adage of "attitude is contagious" is true for both the positive and the negative—we strongly recommend that you limit the time spent commiserating with these folks and absorbing their negativity.

It is our sincere hope that these self-talk skills help you not only in delivering consistently excellent customer service but in your life outside of work as well. Much research shows that positive emotional states have a tremendous impact on your overall health and well-being so we can comfortably say that applying these skills is truly a win-win for everyone involved—you, your company, and the customer.

3

LISTENING SKILLS

Skillful listening is the second Golden Rule fundamental. It plays a crucial role in several aspects of a customer interaction, including serving as a key building block for the Platinum Rule skills explained in Part II. In fact, skillful listening is a critical part of virtually every customer service interaction regardless of the circumstance. This chapter focuses on all the elements of skillful listening and is organized in four parts:

1. Why is listening so important?
2. Listening: the untaught skill
3. The four keys of listening
4. Listening watch-outs

WHY IS LISTENING SO IMPORTANT?

Listening is an important part of your job as a customer service professional for many reasons. Taking the time to listen to your customers helps you understand what they need, helps you build a rapport with them, and helps you solve their problems.

Understanding Your Customer's Needs

First and foremost, listening well allows you truly to understand your customer's needs. We have dealt with many customer service professionals who don't seem to know the importance of listening. Often they're impatient, distracted, or angling to sell the most expensive product in their catalog, no matter what their customer might really need. John experienced this firsthand when he recently decided to buy a new television. After determining what size he wanted and how much he wanted to spend, he headed to the store. Once he arrived in the TV section of the store, a customer service representative greeted him. He told the rep, "I'm here to look at new TVs." Before John could get specific, the rep immediately took him to the largest, most cutting-edge—and therefore most expensive—flat-screen TV on the showroom floor. "Everyone is buying this model," he told John, "because it's the superior product." Then he began to describe all the TV's features. John was already annoyed that the rep didn't let him specify his preferred size and price; then, listening to the pitch, he became truly frustrated. It seemed that the rep was concerned less with John's needs than with making money. John left that store empty-handed. He resolved to try another store, hopefully one with customer service professionals who were better listeners.

Demonstrating Respect and Building Rapport

Excellent listening is one of the most powerful ways to demonstrate respect to another person. If you listen well, you verbally and nonverbally communicate, "I am focused only on you. You are the most important person to me at this moment. Your thoughts and needs matter to me, and I'm committed to learning clearly what they are, so that I can do my best to serve you." Displaying this kind of respect often increases your customer's trust in you. This trust can build even if you are listening to someone for the very first time. Perhaps you have experienced this kind of listening before. Maybe you were at a social event and found yourself talking with a stranger, and yet having a deep discussion. During the chat you felt relaxed and at ease, and you walked away thinking, "I can't put my finger on it, but I really like that person." Many times the hidden ingredient of the successful interaction was your conversation partner's ability to listen well.

Naturally, excellent listening also has a positive effect on customer service interactions. Considering that our goals are to create trust, build relationships, and facilitate positive experiences for our customers, you can see why we place such an emphasis on listening.

Problem Solving

Skillful listening is of paramount importance when you need to solve a problem. It diffuses negative emotions while allowing you to understand a particular client's specific needs, thus giving you the best chance of resolving the situation successfully. This aspect of listening will be our focus.

The Cost of Not Listening

Skillful listening has many benefits. Poor listening, on the other hand, can completely derail a customer service interaction. Research has shown that clients can put up with customer service professionals having a different point of view from their own. They also can deal with not always getting exactly what they want. They won't, however, tolerate not being listened to at all. Skillful listening is not simply a nice thing to do; it's a courtesy we must extend to our customers.

LISTENING: THE UNTAUGHT SKILL

We hope you agree that listening skills are a vital part of being an excellent customer service professional. What percentage of your time do you spend listening to customers? It's probably fair to say that listening takes up a minimum of 60 percent of your time on the job. If we accept this estimate, then more than half your time is devoted to practicing a skill that is vital for success. Now ask yourself this question: Throughout your formal education and training, how many courses have you taken that specifically focus on listening skills? If you're like most of us, you will have taken very few, if any.

Why haven't we had more training in the skill of listening when we spend so much time doing it, and when it's so crucial to our success? The reason is because we believe that we learn this skill naturally, without instruction. "Listening is easy," people sometimes say, "so why would we need training in it? How much can there really be to listening?" A lot! Listening, if it's done well, is a sophisticated skill with very specific steps. Those who are practiced in these steps are the best and most effective listeners. All listening is not created equal; it's a skill that must be developed, just like the other tools of good customer service and it requires great patience and concentration. To see how listening skills can vary, think about your personal experience. For example, when you want to share a success, or if you're going through something difficult and need advice you may notice that you confide in certain friends and family members more frequently. This is no accident. Although all your friends and family may love you and have your best interests at heart, some of them are simply better listeners. Similarly, the customers to whom you skillfully listen to are far more likely to return to your business or increase the amount of their tip.

THE FOUR KEYS OF SKILLFUL LISTENING

Skillful listening is truly a gift: It requires energy, time, and concentration to give, and it helps the customer get what she wants. There are four elements to skillful listening:

1. The Gift of Attention
2. The Gift of Curiosity
3. The Gift of Open-Ended Questions
4. The Gift of Restatement

The Gift of Attention

Once on an out of town trip, Ben decided to try a restaurant recommended to him by a friend. When he returned to his hotel in the evening, he went to the concierge to book a reservation and get directions to the restaurant. The name of the restaurant had escaped him, but he was hoping that if he gave enough descriptive details, the concierge would figure out the place he was looking for. As Ben approached the desk, the concierge was busy working on her computer. He waited for a few seconds, but she didn't look up or acknowledge him. Finally he asked, "Excuse me, would you please help me locate a particular restaurant?"

She glanced up at him briefly: "Sure, what's the name of it?" Then she immediately looked back down at her computer.

A little annoyed at the lack of eye contact, Ben responded, "Well, that's my problem. I don't remember. I was hoping that if I told you what I know about it, you might know its name."

"Uh-huh," she mumbled in reply, eyes still locked on her monitor. Ben was getting a little frustrated, but he continued: "OK, well, it's a Brazilian restaurant that serves a large variety of meats in an all-you-can-eat style." Ben waited for the concierge to reply, but she did not. He continued, "I also understand they have a large salad buffet." The concierge looked up now, but not at Ben;

she greeted a coworker who was passing by. Then she looked back down at her screen again.

Now Ben felt ignored and disrespected. He stopped his description and said, "Are you listening to me?"

This got her attention; she looked up, startled, and said, "Yes, I was listening, and it sounds like you are looking to go to ..." and she named the restaurant.

Ben replied in frustration, "I think you are right about the restaurant; it sure didn't seem like you were listening." He walked away. "Next time I'll try the front desk," he said to himself.

Like the concierge Ben encountered, you might be able to absorb what a person has said without making eye contact, or while multitasking. However if you are not offering your undivided attention—which you demonstrate by focusing solely on that person—you are likely to leave the person feeling that he or she is not your top priority, that you aren't paying attention, and, possibly, that you are rude.

Patience is perhaps the single most important requirement when it comes to paying attention. You must be willing to take the time to face the customer, make intermittent eye contact, and maintain a high level of attention without becoming distracted. This may seem obvious but many factors can easily result in distraction if you're not careful. In today's world, many of us work on computers of some kind. We have walkie-talkies, cell phones, and pagers that may go off at any time. Some of us also work in environments with potential distractions such as TVs, noise, or other people. This all requires a conscious effort to stay focused.

Paying attention is the foundation of great listening, but we often take it for granted, and therefore don't focus on practicing it. If we pay attention, we can get a customer interaction off to a great start.

The Gift of Curiosity

The second key facet of skillful listening is the demonstration of curiosity. It's important to let your customer know you are interested and curious about what he is saying. Have you ever had the experience of talking to someone who is expressionless? This person might look directly into your eyes and doesn't interrupt you, but is not reacting physically or verbally to what you're saying. Although inscrutable expressions are great at the poker table, having to talk to someone with a poker face makes most people uncomfortable at best and irritated at worst. When we ask individuals in our seminars how they feel about being listened to in this way we commonly hear statements such as:

- It left me wondering if anybody was home inside his head!
- I wasn't sure if she was actually listening to me.
- I thought I was boring him.
- It made me feel as though what I was saying was stupid.

So, while paying attention is necessary, you also need to show your customers, both verbally and nonverbally, that you are interested and curious in what they are saying. Some basic ways to demonstrate curiosity nonverbally include:

- Nodding your head
- Changing your facial expression to acknowledge that you understand what the customer is saying (respond to enthusiasm with a smile; to disappointment with a more serious expression)

Verbal demonstrations of curiosity include:

- I understand.
- Oh, I see.

- Yes.
- Got it.

Demonstrating curiosity both verbally and nonverbally reassures customers that you are sincerely interested and that you are following what they say. Consequentially the customers are likely to feel relaxed and at ease—you will win their trust and they will feel they can be open with you.

The Gift of Open-Ended Questions

The third element of excellent listening is the art of the open-ended question. Open-ended questions communicate curiosity, which helps build trust, create openness, and foster receptivity. Open-ended questions also serve a deeper purpose: They let you learn in detail the customer's needs. Many customers will not automatically reveal these details; your careful open-ended questions can help you discover them. For example, you might greet the customer with a warm smile and ask, "How may I help you?" In return, the customer may give you only cursory information. Responses such as, "I'm looking for a vacation package," "I need a new refrigerator," or "I would like a new cell phone," let you see the big picture but not the specifics. Rather than settling for this limited information, we strongly recommend utilizing a few open-ended questions to glean more information. Gathering more detailed information serves you in the following ways:

- Your discussion and discovery of your customer's needs is likely to be far more efficient.
- Asking open-ended questions conveys your intention to focus on the customer's needs and agenda.
- You avoid wasting time or frustrating your customer by inadvertently focusing on the wrong aspects of the product.

Some examples of open-ended questions are:

- Can you tell me more about that?
- What are you most hoping to get out of this?
- What is your main priority when using this?
- What is your ideal (vacation, meal, experience)?
- Historically, what has been your greatest frustration with this?

It is important to make sure that you are asking truly open-ended questions. Truly open questions, like the ones listed above, do not reveal a point of view, thereby giving customers the confidence to be open about their own perspective. Conversely, some questions will reveal your point of view and these are generally not helpful.

- Don't you want to see our top-of-the-line product?
- This is our most popular package; would you like to see it?
- Wouldn't it be best if you...?
- Why don't you take a look at...?

When you ask a point-of-view question, you risk your customers thinking you are giving advice and direction before they have asked for it. If the opinion in your question is contrary to theirs, customers may think you are criticizing them. We recommend you avoid these kinds of questions.

The Gift of Restatement

The final component of good listening is the skill of restatement which means periodically rephrasing your customer's message in your own words. Restatement, when applied effectively, serves two important purposes:

1. It lets the customer know you understand his or her needs—you are conveying the message, "I am truly listening to you.

I understand what you are looking for. I am focused on your needs and not my agenda." Your receptiveness usually puts your customer at ease and builds trust.

2. It ensures that you've correctly interpreted the customer's message as restatement gives the customer the opportunity to correct you if you inadvertently misunderstood. Early clarification eliminates customer frustration and saves you time you might have spent focusing on the wrong issue.

The steps to successfully practicing restatement follow:

1. Give your full attention.
2. Avoid interruption.
3. Wait for a natural pause in the customer's speech, and then summarize what you've heard in your own words.

Some good phrases to use when practicing restatement follow:

- Let me see if I've understood. You're saying that...
- So your request is...
- So you were expecting...
- If I have it right, your main priority is...

Don't restate every one of your customer's sentences and be sure to use your own words. If you parrot customers, you risk annoying them and making them wonder, "Is there an echo in here?" Also, don't restate simple and obvious questions—if a customer asks, "Would you please direct me to the restroom?" there's no need to reply, "So, what I hear you saying is that you want to go to the restroom."

PUTTING IT ALL TOGETHER

The example below illustrates all the listening skills we have covered so far. As you read it, note the various ways this spa receptionist applies the four skills: paying attention, demonstrating curiosity, open-ended questions, and restatement.

A man enters a spa. He approaches the counter, and the customer service professional greets him with a smile.

Spa Receptionist, in a welcoming voice: "Good afternoon, sir; how may I help you?"

Customer: "I'm here for a treatment, but I'm not exactly sure what I want."

Spa Receptionist: "OK, what is it that you're hoping to achieve with the treatment? Is there any particular outcome you are looking for?"

Customer: "Well, I want to end up feeling very relaxed. I need something that's not over an hour long and that won't take all my energy, because I'm going to dinner later."

Spa Receptionist, waiting for the customer to pause: "So you are looking for a treatment with a focus on relaxation, but nothing too intense?"

Customer: "Yes, exactly, preferably some kind of a massage."

Spa Receptionist, waiting again for a natural pause: "So you'd like a massage that's less than an hour long and that will relax you without putting you out for the night."

Customer: "That's it. Do you have something like that?"

Spa Receptionist: "Sir, I have a treatment tailor-made for you: our 45-minute Swedish massage."

Customer: "Perfect, that's exactly what I'm looking for!"

Let's take a look at what the receptionist did well. Firstly, he smiled warmly and spoke in a positive tone. While we couldn't see the spa receptionist's facial expressions, he demonstrated curiosity through questions such as "What is it that you're hoping to achieve with the treatment? Is there any particular outcome you are looking for?" This qualifies as a true open-ended question;

it's neutral and doesn't reveal an opinion. He used this question to solicit the customer's priorities. Then, he skillfully restated the customer's needs to let him know that he was paying attention, while simultaneously confirming that he understood the situation correctly. His two key restatements were: "So you are looking for a treatment with a focus on relaxation, but nothing too intense?" and "So you'd like a massage that's less than an hour long and that will relax you without putting you out for the night." Both of these restatements meet the criteria: they were brief and in the spa receptionist's own words. As well as ensuring he correctly understood the customer's needs, the restatement also allowed him to offer perfectly timed advice on which treatment the customer might enjoy. After having listened so skillfully, the spa receptionist's strong suggestion, "Sir, I have a treatment tailor-made for you: our 45-minute Swedish massage," was a gift to the customer: At this point, the customer clearly felt that the receptionist had heard him, understood his needs, and made a suggestion that fit his agenda.

LISTENING WATCH-OUTS

The more you practice the four listening skills, the more quickly you become an expert listener. Next, you need to decrease—or even better eliminate—the behaviors that most commonly undermine quality listening. The four main listening watch-outs are listed below. As you read them, think about whether you may be engaging in some of these behaviors. We also recommend that you gather additional feedback by asking a few coworkers if they have noticed you inadvertently exhibit any of these behaviors.

Interrupting

You could interrupt a customer in any number of ways if you are not careful. For example, you may be in a particular customer service role in which you are frequently asked the same questions. Because you can predict the question before your customer completes it, you may be tempted to jump in and, although you have good intentions, end up interrupting the customer. Furthermore, you might be a fast-paced person who tends to interrupt when you know the answer or have something to say. Interrupting your customers can make them feel like you are hurrying them, that you are rude and disrespectful, or that you're not fully focused on their needs.

There will, of course, be occasions when you actually need to interrupt a customer. If interruption is necessary, the key is to interrupt in a way that causes customers to feel as though you're still focused on them and their needs. Perhaps a customer describes his needs so extensively that you cannot hold all the details in memory. In this instance, some possible phrases that will allow you to interrupt without offense include the following:

- Excuse me, ma'am, sorry to interrupt, but I just want to make sure I'm following you.
- Sorry to interrupt, sir, but I just want to double-check that I've clearly understood what you have said so far.

Some customers may strike up a friendly conversation when you need to move on to other customers. Here is a phrase that will help you do so graciously: "Sorry to interrupt, sir. I enjoy speaking with you, but I have to attend to my other customers. If I have the opportunity, I'll be back to talk further." Such phrases reassure your customers that the focus is still on them, that you are interrupting only to make sure you can serve them in the best possible manner, and that you respect and value them.

Diverting

The second listening watch-out is *diverting*—changing the focus from the customer to you. If you can do it briefly, relating to your guest can be a positive way to build rapport. For example, if a customer tells you she is from California, it would be appropriate to say something like, "Really? I was born there" and then turn the attention back to her. If, however, you say, "No kidding. You know, I'm originally from California; San Diego to be exact. I lived there until I was nine, and then my parents moved us to New Jersey. It sure was difficult adjusting to the winters," you are diverting and monopolizing the conversation, and you may aggravate the customer.

Monologuing

Many times customers will ask you questions about your product, and sometimes about you personally. It's important to answer the questions thoroughly, but you must be careful not to monologue, or talk for an extended time without interruption. Even if you are answering a question, try not to speak for too long before shifting the focus back to the customer. If you must explain something extensively, you should at least stop periodically and ask questions such as the following:

- Do you have any questions so far?
- Has my explanation been clear?
- Am I focused on your area of interest?

Giving Advice Too Early

As a customer service professional, you frequently field questions about what to choose, where to go, what is the best product, and why that's the case. Not only is it appropriate for you to give your customers advice, it's also a crucial part of your role. However, please be careful not to give advice too early. This can frustrate the customers and make them think you are impatient and not focused on their needs. John's attempt to buy a new television is a classic case of this scenario. Before John could tell the customer service professional what he was specifically looking for, the agent was already advising John on the best product and what he should buy. The representative probably meant well and likely was instructed to tell customers about that particular product. Nonetheless, because the advice came too early in the interaction it had a negative result. It is important to be aware of this tendency. You may sometimes want very much to let your customer know about packages or products you offer. Remember, though, that customers do things for their reasons, not yours. If you give them advice before they feel you've heard and accounted for their reasons, they may feel you are trying to get them to do things for your reasons and not theirs.

You can use your listening skills to ensure that you avoid giving advice too early. Pay full attention, ask open-ended questions, and restate your customers' concerns, and you will avoid seeming as if you are pushing or rushing them into a decision based on your agenda and not theirs. In fact, when a customer really feels you have heard and understood that, that customer often will solicit your advice, as the spa customer asked for the receptionist's.

In conclusion, we realize that, depending on your customer service role you may be in a very fast-paced environment. When you have limited time, efficiency is crucial. We are not asking you to become counselors or therapists, or insisting you spend 15 minutes with each customer. In fact, it usually only takes a few minutes to practice skillful listening and reap all its benefits. The quality of your listening during this short time can make or break an interaction.

Fortunately, there are countless opportunities to hone your listening skills. You can practice listening skills virtually every time you interact with someone, including coworkers, friends, and family. We assure you they will appreciate it just as much as your customers do.

4

PROBLEM SOLVING

The third facet of the Golden Rule is the ability to problem solve skillfully. In a perfect world, you and your customers would always agree, and they would never be dissatisfied with your product or experience. Unfortunately, this isn't always so. There will be times when you and a customer arrive at an impasse: He asks you for something you cannot give him, or he is dissatisfied in some way. It is in these moments that you must employ your problem solving skills. Your skillful handling of these situations is critical to your success as a customer service professional. The primary goal of problem solving is to find an alternative way to meet the customer's needs while still staying within your company's policies and procedures. When this is not possible your goal is saying "no" in a way that minimizes its negative impact on the interaction. When you use problem solving skills well the outcome is almost always positive: either you successfully find a solution that works for you and the customer or if you don't, your customer will see that you have made every effort to meet his or her needs. In the following pages we break down the steps of successful problem solving.

Problem solving skills include the following four steps:

1. The problem solving mind-set—self-talk
2. Empathy
3. Problem solving listening
4. Win-win vocabulary and the soft no

THE PROBLEM SOLVING MIND-SET—SELF-TALK

The first step on the path to successful problem solving is achieving the right state of mind. The idea of never saying no to a customer has become so powerful in the service industry that we may panic if we have to say that dreaded word—we might believe that there can be no positive outcome under these circumstances. Without skillful self-talk we may hold the false belief: "If I can't give this customer exactly what she wants, this interaction is bound to end badly." Given the discussion in Chapter 2 on self-talk, what behaviors do you expect this thought to produce? If your mind-set is negative and you believe you will fail, you feel frustrated and hopeless. In our seminars we have heard many participants describe how this way of thinking can lead to negative self-talk such as, "I'm stuck. If I say yes to the customer, I'm in trouble with the company, but if I say no, I'm in trouble with the customer!" These types of thoughts can create defensiveness. Your frustration may show up in your facial expression and body language. Your listening skills are likely to decline dramatically—what's the point of listening, you may think to yourself, when you see no chance of a positive outcome? Your tone of voice probably also communicates your negative feelings. If you display this kind of behavior, you can almost guarantee that the interaction will go badly. As you can see, negative self-talk can create a self-fulfilling prophecy.

This mind-set is erroneous, and it's negative. It's true that the customer would be happy with a simple "yes" to his or her request. However, it is wrong to assume that your customer will be dissatisfied to not get exactly what he or she wants. Many other factors contribute to a customer's satisfaction. We planted the seed for this idea in Chapter 3 when we cited research indicating that customers can deal with not getting exactly what they want, but no customer can deal with not being listened to. Below is a list of the other components that contribute to customer satisfaction.

- *Friendliness.* Customers want to be treated with a positive attitude and respect.
- *Understanding.* Customers want to feel that their needs and feelings are clearly understood.
- *Effort.* Customers want to feel that everything possible is being done to meet their needs.
- *Fairness.* Customers want to feel that they are being treated fairly.

If you demonstrate all of these traits—and practicing the Golden Rule fundamentals will ensure that you do—you always have the chance of a positive outcome, even if you cannot give a customer exactly what she wants, and even if she is dissatisfied with your product. Your customer's receiving exactly what she wants is not the only determinant of whether she is satisfied. She may be very satisfied by the interaction even if she doesn't receive exactly what she requested. It's equally possible that a customer may receive what she asked for, but still have a negative experience. John experienced both of these scenarios in the past year.

Example 1: Getting What You Want and Not Being Satisfied

On a Friday evening after three days of seminars in Detroit, John was standing in line at an airline ticket counter. The airline personnel announced that John's flight was oversold and that he had been bumped off it. John had an important family event to attend the next morning and it was urgent for him to be there. John asked to speak to a customer service representative, and was directed to Gate 17 where customer service employee Sally sat at the counter. She looked up at John briefly, said, "Yes?" then turned back to her computer screen.

John: "The 6:30 PM to Baltimore has been oversold and I have been bumped, but it is really important that I get on that flight."

Sally, still focused on her computer screen: "Sorry, sir, I can't get you on that flight."

John, perturbed by the lack of attention: "I paid for my ticket for that flight; it's not my fault that you oversold it. I really need to get on that flight."

Sally, with an annoyed look: "I don't make the policies, sir."

John, becoming frustrated: "That helps. Well, what are you going to do for me?"

Sally, looking down at her screen: "Here is what's available. There is a 9:30 PM tonight, and our earliest flight tomorrow is at 8 AM."

John: "I'll take the 9:30 PM."

Sally, looking back down at her screen: "OK, I've got you on it. Can I help the next customer?"

John walked away, frustrated, and sat down in the waiting area. Ten minutes later, he heard his name being called over the intercom, with instructions to go see a customer service representative. The representative informed John that a family had decided to take a travel voucher for a free flight in the future, which meant that he could now take his original flight.

Although John was relieved, he was so dissatisfied with the way he was treated that he vowed to avoid that airline in the future. Although he got what he wanted, he felt that the airline representative treated him unfairly, did not make an effort to help him or understand his problem, and was unfriendly.

Example 2: Not Receiving What You Want but Still Being Satisfied

John arrived at the Jacksonville, Florida, airport on a Tuesday afternoon. He was flying to Chicago, where he was to teach a seminar the next day. When John arrived at the gate, he was informed that once again, his flight had been oversold and he had been bumped. He was told to go see a customer service representative at Gate 12. As John made his way over to the gate, he thought about the amount of time that had gone into planning this seminar, the time he had invested in preparing and customizing it, and the participants who were flying in from many parts of the country to attend. As he approached Gate 12, customer service representative Jeff greeted him.

Jeff, with a smile and welcoming tone: "Good afternoon, sir, how may I help you?"

John: "The 4:30 PM to Chicago was oversold. I was sent here to gather more information."

Jeff, in a sincere tone: "First of all, let me say that I understand what an inconvenience it can be to be bumped off a flight. I wish we could prevent this from happening. Please tell me a little more about your situation."

John: "I need to get to Chicago for a seminar tomorrow morning. It's been planned for several months and most of the participants are flying in from around the country. I need to get on that flight."

Jeff: "Sir, so it's critical that you get to Chicago tonight?"

John: "Yes, that's right."

Jeff: "Well, sir, as a result of our company's policy, I am afraid I'm unable to get you on that particular flight, but if you are open to it, I would like to brainstorm other possibilities to get you into Chicago this evening."

John: "OK, sure. I'd rather be on a direct flight as long as it gets me in before 10 PM. I would rather not have a layover."

Jeff: "If you give me just a minute, I will look at all the possible combinations of flights, and then we can decide on the best option for you. You'd like a direct flight that gets you in before 10 PM, and if that isn't available, you'd like a flight with only one stop—is that correct?"

John: "Exactly."

Jeff enters information into the computer.

Jeff: "OK, sir, I have your options here, beginning with all the direct flights that will get you in before 10 PM, and then the one-stop flights that will get you in earlier."

John, looking over the options: "Thanks for the alternatives. The 7:30 PM direct flight looks like the best. It should get me in right at 10 PM."

Jeff: "OK, sir, I'll get you booked on that right away. I apologize again for the inconvenience."

John: "That's OK; I realize it isn't your fault and it's company policy. Thank you for your help in finding a good solution."

Even though John didn't get exactly what he wanted, he was very satisfied with the service he received. He was so impressed with Jeff's friendliness, understanding, effort, and fairness that he now makes a point of choosing this airline as often as possible. Because Jeff did such an excellent job of applying problem solving skills, we will refer back to this example as we continue.

We hope these examples have convinced you that you can still have an excellent interaction even if the customer asks you for something you initially cannot provide. The first step toward increasing the odds of this kind of interaction is consciously generating the right state of mind. Here is a list of positive self-talk phrases to help you on your path:

- This is an opportunity. I can use my skills to turn this into a positive experience.
- I'm committed to doing my best to work toward an agreement that will work for the customer while using my skills to meet her expectations in all other facets of our interaction.
- Even though I may be unable to give the customer exactly what he wants, I can learn about his needs and use my skills to meet them, making this a positive experience.

We strongly recommend you use phrases like these to enhance your problem solving abilities. Jeff clearly practiced positive self-talk when interacting with John. As a result, his friendly smile and sincere tone got the conversation off to a great start. He maintained that attitude and his composure throughout the interaction.

EMPATHY

Empathy is particularly important when interacting with a guest who is dissatisfied with a product or feels as though he has the right to something you cannot offer. It's one of the best ways to demonstrate understanding. We sometimes find that our seminar participants resist showing empathy, because they feel it means they are admitting fault. Empathy does not mean you must agree with your dissatisfied customers. In fact, you can simultaneously disagree and empathize with them. The word *empathy* literally means, "to see through someone else's eyes." Empathizing with your customers simply means the willingness to see things from their perspective and reflecting this back to them. A customer who sees that you are truly hearing and considering his feelings and point of view will feel much better about the interaction with you and will be more likely to remain calm.

The first step to demonstrating empathy is the use of appropriate facial expressions, such as a look of concern. If you have a blank expression, or worse, look amused while the customer is talking, you are likely to add fuel to the fire and end up with an upset customer. Naturally, a compassionate tone of voice is also important and your body language should be open and friendly. Statements of empathy include:

- Sir, I get very frustrated myself when I feel I have been overcharged.
- I know the feeling of not getting what I expected; it's very disappointing.
- I know the aggravation of feeling like you aren't being listened to.
- I see what you mean.

Jeff, the airline representative, used these empathetic phrases: "First of all, let me say that I understand what an inconvenience this is for you, and I really wish it didn't happen," and "I apologize again for the inconvenience." The first statement immediately let John know that Jeff was concerned and that he understood how John felt. When Jeff apologized for the frustration—which is, again, not accepting blame—he conveyed sincerity and understanding.

PROBLEM SOLVING LISTENING

Your listening skills are a very important part of successful problem solving. We have discussed the importance of paying close attention and demonstrating curiosity, which will put your customer at ease and create trust and receptivity. You can also determine your customer's needs and priorities by using open-ended questions. Jeff asked John to "tell me a little more about your situation." John's response gave him key information to factor in to how he approached John from then on.

Restatement helps you clarify your customer's needs. Remember, you are working toward finding a creative solution to a problem, so it is crucial to discover the customer's top priority. Jeff restated what he perceived to be John's needs as follows: "Sir, so it's critical that you get to Chicago tonight?" and "You'd like a direct flight that gets you in before 10 PM, and if that isn't available, you'd like a flight with only one stop—is that correct?" When John confirmed Jeff's perceptions, he knew exactly what to offer in order to solve the problem.

WIN-WIN VOCABULARY AND THE "SOFT" NO

Win-win problem solving is based on the premise that there is more than one way to resolve a problem. Furthermore, if two parties (individuals, organizations, or countries) are willing to let go of what they perceive to be their only option and consider other solutions both sides can come to a satisfying conclusion.

We recommend applying this principle when solving a customer's problem. Often when a customer asks you for something you cannot provide, the customer sees only one way of getting what he or she wants. If you can invite a customer to have an open mind and explore alternatives you may be able to create a win-win solution. By using positive self-talk to maintain a good attitude, empathy to ensure that the customers feel understood, and listening skills to deepen trust and to gather and clarify key information, you put yourself in a prime position to find win-win solutions. In Jeff's case, he demonstrated to John that he was trustworthy, understood John's feelings, and, most importantly, he figured out John's real need—getting into Chicago by 10 PM that night.

Learning the customer's core need is a key part of the problem solving process and gives you the opportunity to find a win-win solution. Different people have different priorities: They may value speed, reputation, exclusivity, or price, just to name a few. Often, they don't express their core need in their initial request. That is why it is important to gather this information through open-ended questions and then restate it to be sure you have accurately identified the problem.

The best way to engage the customer in win-win problem solving is by using win-win vocabulary. Jeff used an excellent win-win phrase when he said, "Well, sir, as a result of our company's policy, I'm afraid I cannot get you on that particular flight, but if you are open to it, I would like to brainstorm other possibilities to get you to Chicago this evening." We realize that using a phrase like this means telling the customer that you cannot provide exactly what she is seeking. In John's first flight experience, Sally didn't look for a win-win solution or use the correct vocabulary. She said, "Sorry, sir, I can't get you on that flight," and, "I don't make the policy." However, if you know that you truly cannot provide what your customer is asking, it's not a good idea to avoid saying so or try to bend the truth. The customer may feel misled, that you supplied unrealistic expectations, or even that you manipulated him or her.

Win-win vocabulary works like this: Immediately after confronting the reality of the situation, communicate to your customer that you are committed to finding alternative ways to meet his or her needs. This is especially effective when you have listened well to your customer and identified the core need. Jeff identified John's top priority and stated it to him. This put John at ease because he knew that Jeff understood what it would take to solve his problem. After you have practiced the four steps listed at the beginning of this chapter, your use of win-win language will help your customers keep an open mind, and they will appreciate your efforts to help them. Other useful win-win vocabulary phrases include:

- One alternative...
- Another possibility...
- Would you consider...
- What if we were able to...
- Would it resolve the issue if...
- How does this sound...
- An acceptable option for us is...
- I'd like to find a solution that makes you feel better about the situation while still staying within our policy...

If you can apply this strategy and arrive at a solution the way Jeff did, fantastic—you have just transformed a potentially conflict-filled situation into an excellent interaction. On the other hand, even if the win-win discussion does not lead to a solution that's satisfactory for both of you, at least you have made a concerted effort to help your customer. In this case, end your interaction with a soft "no."

The Soft "No"

A *soft* "no" is an empathetic way of telling the customer that you cannot offer what that customer wants. Rather than simply saying "I can't help you," a soft "no" lets the customer know that you are interested in his needs and genuinely want to help but still allows you to stay within the bounds of company policy. Here are some examples of the soft "no:"

- I appreciate your willingness to explore alternatives, and I'm sorry we couldn't come up with a solution that works. Again, here is what I can do for you at this time.
- I'm sorry that this solution doesn't work for you and I regret the inconvenience this has caused you. Unfortunately, the company policy prevents me from meeting your request, but I can offer you...."

In summary, don't panic when your customer is dissatisfied or wants something you cannot offer. Customers evaluate their experience with you on many levels. As long as you practice the customer service fundamentals consistently, you are already handling your customers extremely well. Our proven problem solving formula maximizes your chances of creating a positive outcome under even the most challenging circumstances.

5

CUSTOMERS
ON TILT

Some customers need special attention. As with all our customers, interacting with upset customers effectively still means practicing the Golden Rule fundamentals. Due to their unique nature, however, they require additional consideration. We affectionately refer to these customers as being *on tilt,* poker jargon for a player who is letting emotions and stress get in the way of his or her game, often causing irrational and poor decision making. In the same way poker pros adjust their play when they realize they are playing against an opponent who is on tilt, customer service professionals must adapt to an angry customer. Poker players go on tilt for many reasons, including after losing a costly hand or if another player is talking trash. Few things, however, trigger a player to go on tilt more than experiencing a bad beat. Interestingly, this is also true with regard to your customers.

A *bad beat* in poker happens when a player reads an opponent properly, bets money, and even induces the opposing player to bet with an inferior hand, but then, against the odds, the opponent draws the card needed to win. Many poker players say experiencing a bad beat makes them feel wronged, cheated, and that there is a lack of fairness or justice. Although poker is a game of odds, and therefore somewhat unreasonable to get upset over, this argument doesn't seem so rational to the player at the time.

Similarly, while customers can go on tilt for a variety of reasons, it is usually due to an event that creates the feeling of having been wronged or mistreated. We stress the point that they *feel* they have been wronged. That's their opinion. Just as with the poker player who experienced a bad beat, they may or may not be rational. The difference between the world of poker and that of customer service is this: Poker pros like it when an opponent is on tilt, and they want to keep the opponent there because it gives them an advantage, whereas customer service professionals rarely enjoy dealing with emotionally upset customers, and don't want them to be on tilt. Nonetheless, just as the world's best poker players do with their opponents, we must be able to identify a customer on tilt and adjust our behavior to maximize our chances of success. Poker players use this information to beat their opponents, and customer service professionals use it to best serve their customers.

This chapter includes the following topics:

- Understanding tilt
- Staying off-tilt yourself
- Dealing with the on-tilt customer

UNDERSTANDING TILT

After having worked with thousands of customer service employees, we have found that it is useful to get inside the heads of people who are on tilt because it can increase your chances of effectively serving them. To gain this understanding, we turn to the field of neuropsychology, which has identified two parts of the brain that govern our behavior. One is the forebrain, or the neocortex. Evolutionarily speaking, the neocortex has grown larger over the past five million years and accounts for 80 percent of the human brain's weight. This area of the brain governs logic, reason, long-term thinking, and problem solving. A person operating from the neocortex exhibits the following characteristics:

- Calm and collected
- Relaxed and friendly tone of voice
- Word choice is polite and friendly and may include
  - "Would you consider..."
  - "One alternative I see..."
  - "One possibility..."
  - "From my perspective..."
- Patience
- Good listening
- Openness to others' opinions and thoughts; not defensive
- Looking for a win-win solution to problems

As customer service professionals, we should operate from the neocortex most of the time. In an ideal world, all our customers would operate from their neocortex as well. Unfortunately, this is not always the case.

The limbic system, also known as the *caveman* or *reptilian* brain, is the other behavior-influencing part of the brain. As its nicknames suggest, it is very different than the neocortex. The limbic system is composed of interrelated structures that play a major role in human drives and emotions, such as eating, sleeping, motivation, and memory. This primitive part of our brain has been around for about 200 million years. It directly influences the endocrine and nervous systems, and the brain's pleasure center. It also governs survival, the fight or flight instinct, anger, and fear.

A person operating from the limbic system exhibits the following behaviors:

- Emotionally upset
- Loud voice
- Word choice is aggressive and demanding, such as:
  - "You should…"
  - "You must…"
  - "You have to…"
  - "You never…"
  - "You always…"
  - "You'd better…"
- Impatience
- Interrupts often and doesn't listen well
- Not open to another's point of view
- Goal in an exchange is to win, be right, or hurt someone rather than solve the problem

In other words, a customer operating from his or her limbic system is on tilt. One of the most common places to observe the transition from the neocortex to the limbic system is during rush hour traffic. We've all driven with a calm, even-keeled friend who turned into a raging maniac on being cut off by another car. Limbic drivers might curse, honk the horn, offer the universal salute of displeasure, or try to retaliate against other drivers. In studies, brain function during these stressful situations can be seen to move rapidly from the front to the back of the brain. The results can be disastrous. In 2000, in San Jose, California, a man cut in front of a female driver. She couldn't stop her car in time, and hit the back of his truck. When she pulled over to the side of the road, the enraged man reached into her car, picked up her small dog, and threw it into oncoming traffic. The man was sentenced to prison for felony animal cruelty. You may be wondering, "What was he on? What was he thinking?" What he was "on" was his own limbic system. He wasn't thinking at all—he was simply reacting. This is the point we want to impress on you: Customers on tilt are not thinking rationally or acting normally, and this is because their limbic systems are driving their behavior. The neocortex facilitates critical judgment, while the limbic system is reactionary. Examples of politicians and celebrities speaking and making decisions using their limbic systems are reported almost weekly in the news.

One famous example is actor Mel Gibson's verbal outburst when he was pulled over on suspicion of DUI in 2006, which directly impacted his image, and possibly his future earning potential. Alcohol consumption greatly reduces control of the neocortex.

The same situations can happen with customers on tilt. They are not always sensible—at times they are outright irrational—and their communication style is often unpleasant. They might feel mistreated by your company, they may have been drinking, lost money, missed their flights, got stuck in traffic, had disappointments in their personal lives, or experienced difficulties at work. All these factors can lead to limbic behavior.

KEEP YOURSELF OFF TILT

Now that you understand what causes and drives on-tilt behavior the next step is learning *not* to go on tilt yourself. This can be easier said than done. When someone speaks loudly, aggressively, demandingly, and perhaps is also critical of you, this behavior might move you into your limbic system. Maybe you have observed a coworker who has been triggered by an on-tilt guest, yet is still trying to solve the guest's problem—both parties speak aggressively, don't listen, are bent on being right and want to prove the other wrong. This behavior makes a problem out of a problem. We recognize it can be challenging to resist being triggered by an upset customer, but it's a crucial part of your job. A poker player may have great intuition, know the game well, and play well as long as things are going smoothly. If, however, the player derails when another player talks trash to get under her skin, or when the player experiences a bad beat, that player will never be successful in the long term. Similarly, your ability to manage your emotions when dealing with an on-tilt customer is paramount to your overall success as a customer service professional.

Learn Your Signals

The first step toward avoiding going on-tilt is paying attention to your triggers. Different things trigger different people—the key is to have a keen awareness of your personal buttons. Some examples of triggers:

- Customers who appear to be talking down to you; for example, "You clearly don't understand what you are talking about."
- Customers who interrupt and don't let you finish speaking
- Customers who raise their voices
- Customers who are overly demanding; for example, "Here is what you're going to have to do."
- Customers who try to threaten or intimidate; for example, "Do I need to talk to your manager about what you just did?"

Identifying your triggers helps you catch yourself before you move into your limbic system. Your body also gives you signs that you are about to go on tilt, such as the following:

1. Feeling warm; that is, hot under the collar
2. Heart pounding
3. Neck and jaw tightening
4. Fast and shallow breathing

The more familiar you become with your body's natural reactions as it begins moving toward tilt, the better you will become at noticing these signals and catching yourself.

Your self-talk also tends to change as you begin to go limbic. "It's always the same with these guys," you may think. "Who do they think they are, talking to me like this?" or "I don't have to stand for this!" Remember, thoughts lead to emotions, which lead to behaviors. This self-talk indicates that you are headed straight for tilt. Although there may be some truth to it, it will only hurt you in these situations. The more aware you are of your personal on-tilt self-talk signals, the better chance you have of using positive self-talk to regain clarity.

Finally, another common signal that you are moving toward tilt is that the quality of your listening declines. Often, as we approach tilt, we are far more likely to interrupt in order, to get our point across, or we are simply waiting to make our point rather than really listening. In this state, our empathy, use of open-ended questions, and restatement skills go out the window.

Calmness Strategies

Once you are aware of your signals and notice them as they occur, you have the opportunity to react strategically. We recommend a combined body-mind approach to stop your progression into your limbic system: deep breathing and positive self-talk. One way to help manage many of your physical reactions is to take deep breaths. As you may have noticed, during times of perceived threat (and an engagement with an emotional customer can give our bodies that impression), we tend to breathe more shallowly and quickly. Breathing slowly and deeply is a natural way of calming your body and signaling to it that you're not in a crisis situation. The key is to bring your breath as far down into your belly as feels comfortable, and then repeat this deep breathing until you can feel your signals shift.

Equally important is choosing positive self-talk to replace your reactive tilt-talk. Some helpful phrases include the following:

- No one pushes my buttons but me. I have a choice in how I react to this customer.
- I'm dealing with a person on tilt; he or she is not fully rational at the moment.

- I understand what it's like to be frustrated; I've been there before myself.
- I don't take this personally; I realize this customer is upset at a situation and not me.
- This is a great opportunity to serve this customer. If he or she leaves here upset, we are likely to lose him or her, and perhaps many more customers.
- I am a professional. I get paid to handle these situations.
- I have the skills to deal with this customer.
- I will not let this guest affect how I treat other guests I meet today.

In summary, if you become aware of your signals, take deep breaths, and choose positive self-talk, you can remain calm when dealing with a customer on tilt. You can then bring this interaction to the best possible conclusion.

BRINGING THE CUSTOMER OFF TILT

The reason we provided a detailed description of a person on tilt is to drive home this point: It's impossible to have a rational discussion with a person on tilt, because he or she isn't thinking rationally. We have seen many well-intentioned customer service professionals try explaining reasonably to an on-tilt customer what it was that customer did not understand, and what his or her options were. Even if it's done calmly, this approach usually only escalates the situation. The key is to help bring the customer back out of the limbic system and into the neocortex, so that the customer is capable of rational discussion. The good news is that you already have the fundamental skills with which to accomplish this task; you just need to apply them a little differently.

Venting

Perhaps the most important skill when you're calming an on-tilt customer is listening. Just as with a calm customer, it's crucial to pay attention in order to get off to the right start with a customer who is on tilt, because it allows that customer the opportunity to vent. Remember, whether or not you feel this customer is behaving rationally, he or she feels wronged and needs his or her grievance to be heard. If you appear distracted, look away, or interrupt, you may add fuel to the fire. Often, the customer will begin to calm down if he or she can speak to someone who is paying attention and demonstrating curiosity, in the way you have learned. Be extra patient and pay special attention to yourself while your customer vents; your self-awareness will ensure that your facial expressions and body language are appropriate.

Empathy

We have already discussed the importance of empathy in a problem-solving situation; it communicates to the customer that you understand his or her feelings. The skills are the same when dealing with a customer on tilt, but you have to apply them in a more concentrated dosage. The most powerful way to draw a customer out of the limbic system is to provide the opportunity for the customer to speak his or her mind while you listen and empathize. It's important to take the time to listen and empathize (which, if done skillfully, rarely takes more than a few minutes) because until you deal with your customer's emotions, it will be very difficult to resolve the problem.

Gather Information and Solve the Problem

Once you have used listening and empathy to calm your customer, you can gather information as to the cause of the upset. You can often discover the problem by listening to him or her vent; however, sometimes people who are frustrated or upset can speak very disjointedly. In this case, you must clarify the problem by soliciting more information. You can do this by asking open-ended questions and restating what you understand to be the problem. When you are clear on the key issues, there are two paths to take: If you can resolve the problem, do so. If not, apply the problem-solving skills you learned in Chapter 4.

CUSTOMER TELLS

6

THE PLATINUM RULE
Treat People the Way
They *Want to Be Treated*

If you want to play at the lower to middle levels of poker, mastering the fundamentals—the rules of the game, the basic odds, player psychology, and mental and emotional discipline—will give you decent results. In the same way, if you can develop the core skills described in Part I, you will deliver excellent customer service and can improve relationships at work and at home.

To reach the higher competitive levels of poker, players need to add the skill of reading their opponents and picking up tells. Imagine two very different poker players. One knows basic mathematics and the relative strength of his hand. The other player knows the same information, but also can pick up on who is bluffing, who's on tilt, who is disinterested in the pot, and who just got a card she was looking for. Which of these players has more information and the flexibility to use it? Who would you bet on? Damon Runyon once said, "The race doesn't always go to the swift, the battle doesn't always go to the strong—but that's the way to bet." (Runyon, 1935) In poker, we bet on the player who is an expert on reading tells. Phil Hellmuth, winner of ten title bracelets and almost $5 million at the World Series of Poker, states, "Success in the game is 70 percent reading people, and only 30 percent reading the cards [understanding the mathematics and technical aspects of the game]." (Navarro, Karlins, 2006)

Similarly, in customer service, if you can notice and react to "customer tells," you will achieve the highest levels of performance. This new competence will enable you to follow the Platinum Rule when interacting with your customers.

THE PLATINUM RULE

The Platinum Rule is quite simple: Treat people the way they want to be treated. Why do we need this rule? Because people are different.

In some basic ways, we are the same, but we are also different in many others. Our families and cultural backgrounds have shaped our habits, behaviors, and expectations. Each customer has unique needs and goals. Each customer may also have a unique reaction to your behavior and communication style.

What does all this add up to? When it comes to delivering world-class customer service, one size does *not* fit all.

In the same way that companies customize their products and services to specific tastes, the Platinum Rule can help you tailor your customer service to the person in front of you.

If we go back to the hotel experience Jovita Thomas-Williams described in the Foreword, you can see that the front desk employee applied the Platinum Rule with stunning results. In order to execute this level of customer service, she needed three skills:

1. *An ability to read tells.* She could notice and interpret Jovita's facial expression and body language quickly and accurately.
2. *A range of behaviors to draw on.* She had a repertoire of approaches to greeting guests and could select the one most

appropriate for this particular situation. Similarly, a good poker player can alter his play depending on game conditions. This is not as easy as it might sound: Many people find it more comfortable to use the same approach over and over again. As the popular expression says, "If the only tool you have is a hammer, the whole world looks like a nail."

3. *A willingness to adapt to someone else's needs or expectations.* There is a decision we need to make in any customer relationship: Are we willing to be flexible and adapt?

If it were easy to apply the Platinum Rule, more people would behave as well as Jovita's front-desk person. In fact, because this caliber of customer service is so rare, the interaction shocked Jovita.

When we first did research for *Customer Tells,* we interviewed employees about their approaches. We found that most used a one-size-fits-all approach more often than they realized.

We are all creatures of habit—they are a powerful force in determining our behavior. The path of least resistance, or our comfort zone, is to stick with established patterns that require the least thought and effort. In fact, our habits are largely automatic and unconscious and they only become apparent when we try to change them.

Let's look at one of the employees we interviewed from the hospitality industry. Within a few minutes of talking to Sarah, we could see that she was friendly and open. She had a wide, genuine smile, a good sense of humor, and she was curious about our work. She told us, "I just assume that everyone is looking for a friendly approach. I really try to get them to lighten up and get on a personal level as soon as I can."

We asked her if this method worked with everybody. "Not right away," she admitted. "Some people are a little shy and standoffish, but I kill them with kindness and eventually I win them over. Down deep, everyone is looking for a friend."

Sarah has many customer service gifts and skills. In fact, she has some qualities that probably can't be taught in a training class.

But she is also falling into some common traps that will hurt her success with customers:

- *One size fits all.* Sarah believes that everyone wants to be treated in the same manner. She would love for this to be true, because that is her comfort zone—the easiest and most enjoyable way for her to operate.
- *Missing signals.* Not everyone is looking for a friend or wants to get personal. Some people are private and some customers are in a hurry. Sarah missed these tells from her customers or if she noticed them she ignored their meaning.
- *Not learning from mistakes.* It's doubtful that many customers told Sarah directly that her approach made them uncomfortable. Given her basic beliefs we don't expect that she would learn from the instances when her approach missed the mark.

Sarah eventually went through Customer Tells Training and learned to read tells, expand her range of approaches, and move out of her comfort zone to meet the expectations of specific customers. At the end of the training, she told us, "I can see now that not everyone is looking for a friend. Some people just want what they want as quickly as possible." Sarah implemented her new learning and quickly found herself having much more efficient customer interactions.

YOUR GUIDANCE SYSTEM TO WORLD-CLASS SERVICE

There are many other fields in which reading tells is a key component of success or competitive advantage:

- Customs agents are trained to detect even small signs of nervousness and deception.

- Psychologists use verbal and nonverbal tells to understand a client's real feelings or conflicts.
- Baseball hitters watch for the different ways a pitcher tips off which pitch he is about to throw. Mike Krukow, a former San Francisco Giants pitcher and current TV announcer, said, "There's a guy right now who takes his hands over his head on a fastball. If he takes them behind his head, it's a breaking ball. I can't tell you who it is without robbing the Giants of an advantage." (Fitzgerald, August 13, 2006)
- Football linebackers study the foot placements of opposing linemen to anticipate a run, pass, or screen play.

The poker professional who reads opponents and the front-line employee who reads customer tells both obtain information and use it as their guidance system. It shows the poker player how to play a specific hand and tells the employee how to treat a particular customer.

The concept of reading customers is a feature of sales training. Most salespeople learn two sayings: people will tell you how to sell them, and people do things for their reasons, not yours.

People Will Tell You How to Sell Them

Good salespeople know that if they look and listen, customers show them how they want to be sold. They choose their sales tactics and decide which words to use by picking up clues about interest levels, hot buttons (issues that can trigger the limbic system), and how the customer is reacting. We discuss these techniques in the next few chapters.

People Do Things for Their Reasons, Not Yours

Successful salespeople know that in order to really understand what motivates someone else, they need to go beyond using themselves as benchmarks. A salesperson who has really embraced this saying looks first for what motivates the customer—what is important to him or her.

In sales, things that are important to your customer can include the following:

- Price
- Convenience
- Time savings
- Quality
- Prestige
- Predictability
- Service
- Responsiveness
- Long-term relationship
- Trust

In customer service situations, all these factors may apply. In addition, we need to discover the customer's idea of a positive experience. Unless you are a mind reader (and if you are, you should consider playing high-stakes poker), the only way to understand the mind-sets of your customers is to pay attention to their tells.

TELLS AND TABOOS

So far, we have focused on the positive reasons for reading tells: to apply the Platinum Rule and meet or exceed customers' expectations. Reading tells can also help you avoid negative experiences, because they yield vital information about how people do or do *not* want to be treated. Depending on a person's background, culture, values, and sometimes the mood of the moment, there are certain behaviors that he or she sees as taboo. If you are unaware of these behaviors, you risk unintentionally offending customers. Not only is it highly likely that they won't return to your place of business, but it's also possible that they will complain to others directly or through the Internet.

For this reason, as you read about the variety of customer tells in Part II, please pay equal attention to the dos and don'ts of approaching each customer.

FOUR TYPES OF CUSTOMER TELLS

In Part II, you will learn about the four key types of tells that make up your guidance system for world-class service:

- In-the-moment tells
- Communication style tells
- Cultural tells
- Third-party tells

In-the-Moment Tells

These tells are similar to the ones a poker player picks up when an open card hits the table. The pro is not watching the card, but watching opponents look at their cards. The player can pick up the reaction: disappointment or excitement.

This chapter deals with understanding how a customer is reacting in the moment. Is the customer interested, bored, impatient, irritable, or pleased? You will learn the twelve reactions that customers experience, and the tells that reveal these reactions. Then we show you how to employ the appropriate responses.

Communication Style Tells

Often a poker player who visits a casino is assigned to an open seat at a table, where he or she plays with strangers. The quicker our player figures out the strangers' styles of play (loose-passive,

loose-aggressive, tight, solid, and so on), the better his or her results will be. This ability to spot patterns and predict behavior is
the hallmark of top-level poker players.

Customer service employees also often deal with strangers,
but they too can learn to gauge each customer's style in a small
amount of time. Customers, like the rest of us, are creatures of
habit. They have their comfort zones, and it's unlikely that they
will adapt their approach to us—they are expecting us to adapt to
them. Customers tend to follow four basic patterns of interaction,
which we refer to as their communication style. Customers are
more predictable than they realize. If we can notice their patterns
and identify their styles, we can find shortcuts to working out how
they want to be treated.

Cultural Tells

Chapter 16 on cultural tells explores culture's power to determine our values, our sense of what is normal, and what we consider taboo or offensive. We hope this discussion will be useful
for all our readers, but it's especially targeted at employees who
consistently interact with customers from different cultures.

You will learn about the tells that indicate norms, values and
taboos, and discover how to become an expert on the particular
cultures you deal with repeatedly.

Third-Party Tells

Many customer service roles consist of ongoing contact with
clients who are part of your business or social network. Chapter 17
on third-party tells will show you how to obtain useful information
about your customers and clients from your network. This data
will help you maintain positive relationships and increase your
ability to deliver exactly what the client seeks.

THE WILL DO

Understanding the four levels of customer tells will reveal the optimal approach to specific customers. But remember, there are two other parts to world-class service; you need to expand your range of approaches and be willing to adapt your behavior to other people and situations. This is the *will do* of customer service excellence. This part is up to you, but we hope to build your confidence in your ability to read tells and to motivate you to use your new guidance system.

7

IN-THE-MOMENT TELLS: CUSTOMER REACTIONS

"My dear Watson, you see, but you do not observe."
—Sherlock Holmes

An in-the-moment tell is a signal a customer gives you about how he or she is feeling or responding to you. The cues can come from body language, gestures, facial expressions, vocal fluctuations, eye movements, or choice of words and expressions. If you can learn to quickly and accurately interpret these signals, you will gain vital information about your customer that can't be obtained any other way. In fact, in some ways, at those moments when you pick up a tell, you may know more about your customers than they know about themselves.

These external behaviors and reactions reveal your customers' true intentions; an outward reflection of their inner feelings. They indicate a wide range of reactions to what you are saying, how they feel about you, the depth of their interest or concerns, or their general emotional state at that moment. Tells can indicate when customers are with you in the conversation or when you have lost them.

Taken together, the In-the-Moment Tells system is your guidance mechanism to how a customer is reacting. As with all customer tells skills, this information, and our ability to shift our approach based on it, increases our chances of minimizing conflict, maximizing comfort, building positive relationships, meeting needs, creating value, and always learning and improving.

The ITM Tells system is described in Chapters 7 through 9. In this chapter, we focus on customer reactions. You will learn why customers give off so many tells, and why they provide such reliable information. Then we explain the twelve most important customer reactions to look for, and many of the specific tells for each type of reaction.

In Chapter 8, Where the Tells Are, we go beyond the specific tells for the twelve reactions and encourage you to become a student of the rich flow of information coming your way from the people around you. You will learn about how to interpret signals from the following:

- Facial expressions
- Eye movements
- Body language
- Gestures
- Voice
- Changes in skin color
- Choice of words/expressions
- Shifts in behavior

Chapter 9, Responding to Tells, gives you the potential payoff for becoming a keen observer of people. You will learn about the three choices you have to respond effectively to what you are seeing in the customer.

1. Quickly adjust
2. Say what you see
3. Learn for the future

YOUR "TELL" IS SHOWING

Why do some poker pros wear sunglasses at the card table?

If professionals—who have trained themselves to mask their reactions at the table—feel the need to prevent their opponents from watching their eyes, think about how much information the average person reveals through his or her eyes.

These players are trying hard not to show their opponents:

- They are upset.
- The card that hit the table was the one they wanted.
- They are nervous.
- They're paying attention to or have lost interest in this pot.

They know almost all their opponents are aware of the probabilities, and that, over time, everyone at the table will get a similar number of quality hands. The difference at this professional level of play often comes down to the extra information gathered through tells.

Research reinforces this fact. When expert poker players had to play against average players who were wearing sunglasses, the number of hands they won decreased. They lost some of the edge they usually gained by observing the dilation of pupils.

By wearing sunglasses, a player acknowledges that she doesn't trust herself to completely control her reactions. For similar reasons, some players remain silent. Scientists have discovered information about voice patterns that justifies this strategy. Howard Nusbaum, chairman of the Department of Psychology at the University of Chicago, conducted experiments showing that people unconsciously gesture with their voices, adding a channel of self-expression that we often don't notice in ourselves, but that those around us pick up. (Nusbaum, 2006)

Fortunately for customer service professionals, most of our customers are not professionally trained in disguising their reactions, voice patterns, and other indicators as to how they feel.

In fact, frontline customer service employees often bear the brunt of customers' unvarnished, uncensored reactions.

As a result, a high percentage of customers are:

- reacting naturally and not trying to disguise their responses;
- likely to have only minimum control over facial, eye, voice, and body language reactions; or are
- unaware of the messages they are sending.

Just like players at a poker table, customers offer us a steady flow of valuable information. We need to know what to notice, how to interpret it, and how to act on it.

We are confident that if you add basic customer service skills to your knowledge of your product, you will be an effective employee. To reach the next level of excellence, however, we encourage you to add the guidance system that comes with noticing customer tells. Just as a guidance system on a rocket continually adjusts the flight pattern so the rocket is exactly on target, reading in-the-moment tells helps you zero in on what your customer is expecting and feeling.

Some people are simply gifted in their talent for reading others. They can follow their intuition about others' emotions, noting whether they seem nervous and deciding if they can be trusted. Others have developed their talents through rigorous training. Poker professionals, customs agents, police interrogators, psychologists, trial lawyers, and top salespeople are all experts at noticing small clues that reveal inner feelings. Their ability is even more remarkable because they often interact with people who are trying to hide their true intentions.

Fortunately, there is hope for those of us who haven't had the rigorous training of a customs agent. Reading in-the-moment tells is a learnable skill, and the people we meet in customer service situations are generally easy to read. We can all improve dramatically if we are willing to focus on others and learn to recognize key patterns.

John Cammack, head of Third-Party Distribution at T. Rowe Price Group, with $90 billion in assets under his management, has systematically taught himself about facial expressions. He credits this knowledge with helping him as a leader and with T. Rowe Price clients. "These are learnable skills, and we can all increase our awareness," he says. "Our team needs to create a better value proposition than our competitors. The key for us is to understand on a deep level what the client really needs. I don't just rely on their words; facial expressions tell me about intentions, commitment, and intensity." (Cammack, 2006)

Research indicates some innate differences in men and women's abilities to notice tells. Dr. Mark Williams, a postdoctoral fellow at the Massachusetts Institute of Technology, and Dr. Jason Mattingley, a psychology professor at the University of Melbourne, Australia, measured men and women's ability to identify emotions conveyed by facial expressions. In general, men were better at picking up expressions of anger. Women were quicker than men to notice expressions of fear, happiness, sadness, surprise, or disgust. (June 6, 2006)

In her book *The Female Brain* (2006), Louann Brizendine says that many factors can strengthen or weaken our ability to read people. Our gender, culture, family circumstances (for example, our birth order), and our different roles and responsibilities may help us in some areas, but not others. With study and practice, this is an area in which we can all improve.

Knowing how people feel, and how your behavior impacts them, has many useful applications. You will be much more attuned to your coworkers, supervisors, friends, and family, as well as your customers. If you live in a state where gambling is legal, this ability will also improve your results at the poker table.

What's the alternative? Perhaps you think you are funny or fascinating. This is fine if you do in fact possess these qualities. However, let's entertain another possibility; perhaps your stories aren't that funny and your comments aren't that insightful. You are not noticing the facial expressions, body language, and side comments that would give you a clue as to your actual impact. This combination of inflated self-perception and refusal to pick up on tells probably will lead to jokes at your expense or nicknames being coined for you. You also are not absorbing feedback that may help you change or improve.

What happens if we don't pick up tells from our customers? Let's say you are talking with a customer, and you fail to notice that he is any of the following:

- Very interested
- Bored
- Impatient
- Surprised
- Frustrated

If your customer is experiencing one of these emotions, or a variety of other possible reactions, and you don't notice, several negative outcomes may occur.

- You will not accurately gauge the customer's needs and expectations, which reduces the chance you will meet them.
- You will probably continue exhibiting the same behavior, and won't make needed adjustments to your words or tone.
- If the interaction doesn't result in a positive experience for the customer, you will be less likely to figure out what went wrong and decide how to improve.

We hope we have convinced you that developing your tells guidance system will pay off personally and professionally.

KEY CUSTOMER REACTIONS

Because there are so many reactions and feelings your customer may have, it's important for us to narrow our focus and highlight what we consider to be the most important behaviors. We have identified twelve key reactions. Understanding these key customer reactions can open up opportunities to provide your clients with exactly what they want, guide you in building and maintaining positive relationships, help you avoid pitfalls, and teach you how to curtail negative interactions.

We describe each of the twelve key reactions, and then explain its importance. Later in the chapter, we list the specific tells associated with each reaction, and discuss how you can choose to respond to them.

1. Interest

Customers' interest and concentration levels often fluctuate during a conversation. Say you are explaining some aspects of your product or service, and your customer is listening politely. You describe one of your product's features, and notice your customer's interest spikes.

This is the most basic factor to monitor in your conversations. Even if we know nothing about a person, his or her interest level tells us what is important to him or her. You can then use this information if you encounter this customer again. You can also see which aspects of your presentation, both in style and content, connect with that customer. Signs of interest include the following:

- Eye contact, turning toward
- Asking questions
- Tracking behavior—head nods, timely comments
- Larger pupil size
- Not doing other things while talking with you

2. Lack of Interest

A person who was talking to his boss, trying to make an important sale, or listening to a close relative, probably would try hard to conceal boredom. He wouldn't want to insult someone important to him. It's unlikely that you, as a customer service professional, are in that category, however. If he is uninterested in what you are saying or how you are saying it, his words, attitude, or body language likely will let you know.

We don't want valuable customers thinking, "Why doesn't she tell this to someone who cares?" We all bore people sometimes—that's unavoidable. Skillful communicators, however, notice when their conversation partners have lost interest. They then learn and adjust. Customers who have lost interest might exhibit some or many of the following signs.

- Less eye contact
- If eye contact is made, a lack of tracking behavior
- Turning away
- Fidgeting
- Interruptions, changing subjects
- No questions
- Blank facial expression
- Looking at watch
- Sighing
- Elbow on table, propping chin with hand
- Drumming fingers on table
- Tapping feet on floor

3. Impatience

This is probably the most common behavior you'll notice in your customers. First, type A personalities (of which there are many) are routinely in a hurry. Second, the pace of life has increased for most of us—our schedules are packed with chores, commitments, and even fun activities. There isn't much we can do to change these causes of impatience. The title of Edward M. Hallowell's bestseller, *Crazy Busy* (2006), sums up the situation.

If we can pick up tells indicating impatience, we can revise our behavior. Maybe we can shorten our explanation, walk a customer to his or her destination, explain how long a service might take, or make a friend by finding ways to save the customer time. Signs of impatience include the following:

- Rapid pace (speech, walking)
- Interrupting
- Finishing others' sentences
- Wanting to skip points
- "Antsy" behavior

4. Something Unexpected

By definition, this is one reaction nobody can prepare for. One main reason a poker pro wears sunglasses is to conceal his surprise at an opponent's bet or a card hitting the table.

Customers can be surprised by a variety of things we say or do. Whether the tell is in their eyes, face, or body language, it is very important information. You'll need to use follow-up questions to determine whether the surprise is a good or a bad one.

Business rules might sometimes surprise a customer. Some examples are pricing policies or protocol that employees and clients must observe. Customers might react to something unexpected with any of the following:

- A jerk of the head or torso
- Raising their eyebrows
- Dilated pupils

5. Anger

You have learned about the power of the limbic system and its impact on how we think and speak. Unfortunately, there are plenty of different situations in which you will have to deal with an angry customer. Customers might be angry about something that happened before you encountered them. They may also be tired, hungry, in a hurry, or have lost or spent more money than they expected.

If you can quickly spot some signs of frustration in its early stages, you can better deal with or even diffuse the situation. Remember, these are the types of situations most likely to get ugly. A customer could become very upset with your organization, and then communicate his dissatisfaction. Anger is often expressed with the following:

- Louder, faster speech
- Less listening, more interrupting
- Finger pointing, balled fists
- Tightened muscles, especially the jaw
- Staring
- Skin turning red
- Cursing
- Exaggerations such as "always" or "never"
- Threats
- Turning away
- Repeated phrases
- Invading personal space

6. Embarrassment

Chapter 16, on cultural tells, will teach you how to understand cultural differences, including the fact that each culture has certain taboos. Rarely would a customer service employee intend to embarrass a client, but it can happen accidentally if he or she is not aware of cultural and personal boundaries. Age gaps and gender differences may also lead to one person underestimating the sensitivities of another. A joke may be taken the wrong way, or a comment may be interpreted as criticism. For instance, the term *young lady*, these days, is often considered patronizing. People also have vastly different boundaries when it comes to touching, what they consider to be appropriate sexual conduct, and what subjects are too personal to ask about or discuss.

Chapter 16 will help you anticipate many customer sensitivities, but we all say or do the wrong thing at some point. If you can notice the signs of embarrassment, you can possibly save face, or at least learn not to make the same mistake next time. These signs include the following:

- Skin reddens
- Withdrawal
- Apologetic behavior

7. Tentative

Sometimes you will deal with tentative people who have difficulty making even the smallest decisions. Other times, a normally decisive person will have trouble making up his or her mind; or perhaps you're dealing with two people who each want different things. Most of us can notice the obvious clues of indecision—or if customers actually tell us they can't decide, we should be listening. There are times, however, when the customer doesn't voice this indecision and instead only gives subtle cues. If you miss them, you may unwittingly pressure your customer, or become impatient and frustrated yourself. You may also miss an opportunity to be empathetic and supportive, which could solidify a longer-term relationship. Signals of a tentative customer include the following:

- Hand gestures indicating "weighing options," "balancing scales"
- Throwaway lines—"This is a no-win situation"
- Puzzled facial expression
- Halting, start-and-stop speech pattern
- Making a point then saying the opposite

- Using qualifying vocabulary: "maybe," "probably," "sort of," "might"
- Stroking the chin

8. Anxious

People who are nervous, anxious, or under stress tend to limit their focus, and they also may not listen attentively. If you miss these signals, you could be explaining an issue or solving a problem for someone who's not really following you, or for whom your comments are not sinking in. However, if you can see the signs of nervousness, you may be able to change your approach, determine the cause of anxiety and deal with it, or display empathy and support. Signs of anxiety include the following:

- Picking at cuticles
- Antsy behavior, tapping, or repetitive behavior
- Frightened, tense facial expressions or knitted brows
- Not picking up on things being discussed
- Pacing
- Hands shaking slightly
- Hands sweating
- Overly rapid, or halting, speech
- Tight smile or nervous giggle

9. Not Clear

Many people never say, "I don't understand," admit confusion, or tell you they don't know what you're talking about. This results in misunderstandings, mistakes, poor decisions, and unnecessary frustration. Why don't people admit to being confused? Sometimes it has to do with cultural norms. Other times, gender is the culprit: Often, men are reluctant to admit they don't know something. Still others believe that admitting confusion makes them seem less intelligent. In any case, this is a key reaction to notice, otherwise you may continue to overload an already puzzled customer with information. Signs of confusion include the following:

- Eyes look glazed over, no spark or energy
- Doesn't exhibit normal reactions to what you say, or doesn't ask questions
- Energy level goes down
- Perfunctory comments such as "uh-huh"

10. Distrustful/Guarded

Most of us see ourselves as trustworthy, of course, and so we might be surprised or even insulted if a customer treats us with suspicion. We might even take it personally. While it's important to eventually learn if this distrust stems from our actions, there are also other possible reasons for it. Some people are normally more guarded. Others may see you as representing the company, view you as an adversary, and decide they can't be too open with you. In any case, it's important to notice these tells. Unless you directly address the issue or modify your approach, you may inadvertently add to the customer's distrust. Be aware that your words may be viewed through a lens of mistrust, and therefore might not get through to the customer. We all listen differently when we don't trust the speaker. A guarded customer might show the following signs:

- Increased physical distance
- Closed body language
- Very little agreement with what is being said
- Short answers
- Skeptical questions
- Hesitant speech patterns
- Sarcastic comments, throwaways

11. Seeking Attention

This behavior is not as crucial to notice as many of the previous patterns. However, if you do notice this behavior and adapt to this need, you will have a much happier and more loyal customer.

Human beings vary a great deal in some central needs. David McClelland was a pioneering psychologist who measured the variance in needs among people and between cultures. He identified important goals, such as the need for achievement, the need for power, and the need for affiliation.

Some customers exhibit behaviors that indicate a high need for attention. This goes beyond just getting a response to their requests. They may want you to notice or comment on something about them. These tells are important to notice, especially in key customers, because if they don't get attention from you, they may seek out someone else to meet this need. Customers who seek attention might exhibit the following behaviors:

- Clothing that is unusual, colorful, or skimpy
- Name-dropping, bragging
- Talking a lot about themselves: "Enough about me; what do you think about me?"
- Fluctuating energy level and interest if focus is not on self
- Many attempts to be funny
- Physically positions self to be center of attention

12. Happy/Excited

It would be great if our customers always displayed these feelings. Our roles would be more pleasant and less challenging. While we hope to induce more of these reactions by using our skills, we are grateful for them no matter how they arise. Because dealing with a happy customer is positive, and maybe even a relief, you may have a natural tendency to relax. This is fine, but we hope you're learning while you are reacting. If you make a mental note of what you are doing right, you can use this information in future interactions with this customer. You can discover what, in particular, the customer likes about your product or service, or gain insight into the customer's personality. A happy or excited customer may show the following signs:

- Smile, laughter
- More inflection in voice
- Eyes, pupils widen
- Standing closer, more touching
- Compliments

Now that you know the key customer reactions you need to be aware of, we will shift our focus in the next chapter to where you are most likely to find tells.

8

IN-THE-MOMENT TELLS: WHERE THE TELLS ARE

Knowing the twelve most important reactions and the tells that indicate them dramatically increases your awareness of what your customers are feeling and what matters to them. In this chapter we want to broaden your understanding of where tells emanate from so that you can continue to expand your powers of observation. Many tells are types of body language that can be found in the face, skin, eyes, hands, and body movements. The voice is another source of tells; not what is said, but *how* it is said. Other tells are found in word choice and changes from normal patterns of behavior.

THE FACE

Facial expressions are an important way for human beings to communicate nonverbal messages. Even though we have highly developed verbal abilities, facial expressions can add emphasis, meaning, or even reveal information we would like to keep hidden.

We start with the face not only because it's usually the first place one looks when meeting a person but also because each of us already has a long history of reading the facial reactions of people around us, starting with our parents. When we do sales training, we often use the quote that "children are the best salespeople." Not only can they be very persistent about what they want but they also can figure out how strong your resolve is. If they sense any weakening in your position, they often quickly move in to close the sale. Of course, then when you say "OK," in a weak moment, they will later remind you, "You promised."

We use this example not only to show you that reading facial cues is a natural and learnable skill, but also to remind you that children study parents because it helps them get what they want. No one taught them to do it. In the average household, children know more about their parents' reactions and state of mind than vice versa.

What happens to this ability as we get older? We always have it and potentially can build on it, but we don't use it as often as we could. If we become too focused on what we want to say or how we feel, or we get too distracted, we are unlikely to notice clues, especially subtle ones.

We all have some competence in reading people. We've all looked at someone's face and commented, "You seem down," or excited, worried, disappointed, or angry. Common, easily recognized expressions convey these feelings. We all can get better at this skill by paying attention to facial expressions while we are interacting.

We discuss eyes and skin color changes a little later. The other important parts of the face are the jaw, mouth, eyebrows, and forehead. When people tighten their jaw, they are not in a good mood. No one does this when they are relaxed and happy. Most likely, a tight jaw indicates anger or displeasure with what you are saying.

The mouth reveals a much wider array of information. The corners may turn down when someone is disappointed with what you are saying or how the process is going. Tight and compressed lips also indicate anger or nervousness—other tells can inform you which it is. When you see someone licking or biting lips, most likely that person is anxious.

Pay particular attention when the customer parts his or her lips, because it may indicate a desire to say something or ask a question. It's a good signal to stop talking.

Probably the most important behavior to notice is smiling or the lack thereof. This is often an unconscious but powerful indicator of how someone is feeling, and in particular how they feel about you.

If you are trying to be funny, or discussing generally pleasant subjects (for example, children, vacations, or celebrations such as weddings, anniversaries, or birthdays), and you see no smiles from those around you, take note. As well as signaling the need for a change in your approach, this reaction probably tells you a lot about your customers.

If customers simply smile politely (with a quick but small up-turning of the edges of the mouth), it may not mean much, but a genuine, wide smile indicates a positive mood and/or a positive reaction to you. Later in this section, we discuss what it means when your customer smiles—or doesn't smile—when normally you would expect one.

Not everyone is animated; of course you will run into poker-faced individuals. Even these people, however, can reveal a lot through their forehead and eyebrows. You might see surprise (raised brows), concern/worry (furrowed brow), or skepticism (brows moving inward and downward).

Changes in Skin Color

The lighter-skinned a customer is, the more this tell will show. While people rarely turn pale (unless they are about to faint), in customer service situations you occasionally see red faces and necks. Even if it doesn't occur that often, it's an uncontrollable reaction and one that may embarrass the customer. This rush of blood to the face and neck is triggered by anger, shame, or a combination of the two. It may be a much more reliable clue to a customer's feelings than what is being said.

Eyes

Most of us have heard the saying, "The eyes are the windows to the soul." When President George W. Bush met with Russian leader Vladimir Putin, he said that he had looked into Putin's eyes and seen his soul. While we are reluctant to make a similar claim, it's true that a customer's eyes can potentially provide more information than any other source of tells. Because many eye movements and reactions are involuntary, they are an important key to a customer's—or a poker player's—thoughts.

We are accustomed to many descriptions of how people look at each other, such as the following:

- She looked daggers at him.
- If looks could kill…
- She had a gleam in her eye.

What sort of eye contact is your customer making—is it an angry stare or a confident gaze? Is the customer uncomfortable or distracted, and looking away? Perhaps he or she is interested or surprised, which can cause the pupils to dilate. Our eyes can appear clear and focused, or dull and glazed with boredom or confusion.

HANDS AND GESTURES

People do so many things with their hands and so many cultures use unique gestures, that it's impossible to describe everything you may encounter. The following are some of the tells you are most likely to see:

- *Making a fist.* Indicates anger and frustration.
- *Picking at nails or cuticles.* May be a habit, but even so, indicates increased tension.
- *Drumming or tapping fingers.* Indicates anxiety or boredom.
- *No hand movement.* Not necessarily a tell about inner feelings, but indicates a controlled person. This can be a sign someone is withdrawing from the conversation but only if other tells point in the same direction.
- *Talking with their hands.* In later chapters on communication style and cultural tells, we come back to this behavior. Pay attention to the picture your customer is painting for you and notice what she emphasizes.
- *Rubbing the jaw.* Indicates someone may be thinking things through and weighing his options.
- *Finger pointing.* More likely to come from a male customer who is frustrated or impatient. Accompanied by certain words, it conveys an actual or implied threat.
- *Throwing their hands up.* This is either a sign of frustration or confusion. Other aspects of the situation should help you decide which it is.

BODY MOVEMENT

A person's body movements combine common human behaviors, habits acquired from family and culture, and the emotions that person is currently experiencing. The following are important elements to notice.

Distance

Almost all of us have a comfort zone in terms of how close we like to stand to people, including strangers. One episode of the television show *Seinfeld* featured a "close talker," a person who intrudes upon another's personal space. It's very easy (and funny) to read the body language of Jerry Seinfeld and his costars as the close talker repeatedly invades their space. The close talker either doesn't read the tells pertaining to his intrusion, doesn't care, or can't break the habit. You don't want your customers to squirm like Seinfeld and his friends, so get a sense of your customers' comfort zones by watching where they position themselves in relation to others.

Turning

Customers sometimes turn toward or away from you. In general, it is better if they turn toward you, signaling they're more engaged and attentive. If they turn toward you to make a point or to ask a question, this subject is more important to them than whatever else you've been discussing. If a customer turns away from you, it is not necessarily negative, but it may indicate a lack of interest in what you're saying.

Jerking Head or Body

Remember that almost no one, except perhaps a spy or master of meditation, can hide surprise. In addition to widening the eyes, the person may quickly jerk his head and sometimes also the torso.

Pacing

Depending on your customer service venue, you may notice customers pacing. This is usually a sign of boredom or tension. Some people express anxiety by becoming *antsy*, a word derived from the phrase "ants in your pants." It's an appropriate metaphor: The person looks like she can't sit still. Antsy people may cross and recross their legs or continually shift in their chairs.

If this type of behavior precedes the pacing, you can assume that the person is walking back and forth because of nervous tension, not boredom.

Guarded Versus Open

Thirty-five years ago, when the study of body language became part of popular culture people probably went too far in thinking it was an exact science. While we have obviously devoted a large part of the book to what body language can tell us, we believe that sometimes people cross their arms because it's a comfortable habit, not because they are defensive or mad. To determine whether someone is putting up his guard, we would note his crossed arms, but we would also see if this gesture is accompanied by other signs such as physical distance, restricted speech, or an impassive or skeptical facial expression.

Open body language is usually indicated by uncrossed arms and legs. The most encouraging posture to see is called "relaxed alertness" in which the other person has open body language, erect posture, and is calmly giving you his full attention.

THE VOICE

All the tells we have described so far are visual tells. As we mentioned earlier verbal clues are also abundant—and, research shows, also partially unconscious. We all display our lack of self-awareness in this area when we listen to a recording of our voice and are surprised by its sound.

It is fortunate that there are so many voice tells, because more and more customer service transactions occur on the phone. While the flow of information isn't as rich as it would be in a face-to-face interaction, many phone employees have found that by focusing solely on voice clues and words tells can be easier to isolate.

Volume

While customers' vocal volume is often variable, it is important. Later in this chapter, we discuss what it means when we hear the volume change, but in general, customers speak louder when they are angry or frustrated.

Inflection

People put inflection in their voices for emphasis and to express emotion.

Tone

We all recognize and react to someone's tone of voice, sometimes more so than the words he or she is saying.

Mom: "I don't like how you are speaking to me."

Child: "I didn't say anything wrong."

Mom: "Don't you use that tone with me, young man."

Because this is a book we can't give you vivid examples of tone. Fortunately, you have been hearing different tones and using them all your life. Listen for extra emphasis and volume a person may use to convey enthusiasm and excitement—or anger and disrespect.

Pace and Fluidity

A customer who speaks rapidly is probably a fast-paced individual who's less patient than the average customer, or he or she is highly emotional. In the latter case, the person is probably angry or nervous. A slow pace might be a customer's normal style of speech, or it could indicate that he or she is relaxed and in no hurry. However, if the customer stops and starts, takes a while to choose the right words, or goes back and corrects him or herself, this could indicate indecision, nervousness, or distrust.

CHOICE OF WORDS

As you learned in the chapter on listening skills, the best information we can gather about a customer's needs and expectations can be acquired through curiosity and good listening. In addition, it's important to note particular phrases a customer may use to indicate stronger emotions or reveal how he or she really feels.

Expressions

Every language has popular expressions or clichés. Some of them indicate what people may be feeling.

- I'm caught between a rock and a hard place.
- Heads you win, tails I lose.
- Who are the geniuses that came up with this plan?

Some expressions may be delivered in a sarcastic manner, which also reveals how the customer feels.

Exaggerations

Exaggeration may be this customer's normal communication style (which we discuss in more detail in Chapter 12). But if you turn to the list of limbic vocabulary in Chapter 5, you will notice that when people start to go limbic, they tend to exaggerate. Listen for phrases such as the following:

- You guys always do this.
- They never get it right.
- This has happened 50 times.

Throwaways

More than a hundred years ago, Sigmund Freud discovered an interesting fact: When people want to say something but think perhaps they shouldn't, they resolve the dilemma by making jokes, sarcastic remarks, or side comments. We call these *throwaways*. The person who utters a throwaway is saying what she wants to say, but acting as if no one is hearing it or as if it's just a joke. Everyone who reads tells for a living—psychologists, salespeople, and poker players—pays special attention to these comments. They are very revealing to a trained ear.

Throwaways may be said as an aside, in a lower-than-usual voice, or in a joking manner. Examples of throwaways include the following:

- I'm positive *that* never happened.
- I'll bet you say that to everybody.
- Where have I heard that before?
- I won't hold my breath.

CHANGES

From the Norm

Fictional detective Sherlock Holmes, famous for his powers of observation and deduction, solved a murder using the change from the norm tell. After an intruder broke into a home and killed someone, Holmes realized that normally when strangers entered this house the dog barked. But the dog had not barked at this intruder, leading Holmes to believe the dog knew the murderer. Changes from the norm are often noticed at the poker table.

The World Series of Poker almost always has some surprising results. More than 8,000 participants competed in 2006, and a relative novice, hedge fund manager David Einhorn, finished 18th, winning more than $650,000. His biggest pot, which cemented his high finish, was won when he called a very large bet and his opponent was bluffing. Einhorn later explained, "I knew he had nothing because of how aggressive he was. It was not the normal way he would play a good hand." (Anderson, August 11, 2006)

Poker players are always looking for deviations from the norm, such as a player's actions when he eats at the table, which during long tournaments many players do. Normally while eating, players give their cards a perfunctory look, throw away poor or marginal hands, and decide against bluffing. If a player looks at her cards, puts down her food, and makes a bet, she is "telling" you she has a good hand.

After working in customer service for a while you develop expectations regarding customer interactions. Even if these expectations include a wide range of behaviors and responses, you regard them as common. These experiences usually include the questions people ask, when they smile, and what they don't like. So when a customer does something different from your expectations, he or she is giving you important information. Is it a sign of cultural difference (described in Chapter 16)? Is it a style difference (Chapters 10 through 15), or an important emotion? By paying attention to this change from the norm you may soon learn how to adjust your approach accordingly.

From This Customer's Norm

In some cases, you see a customer regularly. Just as a poker pro remembers people and patterns of play, great customer service people remember key aspects of their customers' personalities. This helps them predict the best approach to each customer.

Any change from a customer's norm may be significant. If you talk to someone for 10 to 15 minutes, you may get a sense of his or her normal communication patterns. Now you are in a position to notice change. For example:

- Did the customer's pace of talking speed up or slow down?
- Was the customer initially a patient listener, but is now interrupting you?
- Was the customer engaged in the conversation, but is now quiet and withdrawn?
- Is the customer suddenly paying attention and asking questions after a period of seeming disinterested?
- Has the customer been looking away but then stares at you when they are making a point?
- Is it just the opposite—the customer has been looking at you, but now seems uncomfortable making eye contact as you converse?
- Was the customer speaking at a fluid pace, and is now starting and stopping?

These changes can reveal key data you don't want to ignore.

CONGRUENCE

When someone's words, facial expressions, voice, and body language all seem to be sending the same message, we say that person is congruent. Everything hangs together. Often we experience this message as a sincere and credible expression of that person's feelings. Congruent messages may tell us what is of deep importance to our customer.

It isn't unusual to receive incongruent messages. Most of us have had this experience: At the supermarket checkout counter, the grocery bagger hands us our bags, and with a flat voice and no smile, says, "Have a nice day." Somehow, this doesn't brighten our mood.

Customers may say, "Oh, sure. It's fine. Well...no...yeah, it'll be fine." Their faces, voices, and body language are telling you, however, that it's not fine at all. In these situations, the nonverbal cues are much more reliable than the words spoken.

We hope that we have given you enough information and motivation to become more of an expert at picking up tells. If you want to improve, set aside 15 to 30 minutes a day to study tells, in addition to practicing with your customers. Social settings such as movies, TV, meetings, airports, and restaurants offer many opportunities to sharpen your skills.

9

IN-THE-MOMENT TELLS: RESPONDING TO TELLS

The purpose of becoming good at reading tells is to raise your level of customer service. This can only happen if you make the correct changes in your behavior toward the customer in the moment or in the future.

Let's go back to the experience that Jovita Thomas-Williams described in the foreword—the "Aha" moment that led to *Customer Tells*. Remember that the woman at the check-in counter read the tells from Jovita's face, body language, and voice. Knowing that those signals were an outward reflection of her mood and interests, she adjusted her own facial expression and behavior to match Jovita's needs. The reason this behavior stood out so positively is that it isn't as common as we would like.

Following are some other responses we might hear from customer service people in this kind of situation.

- *Not noticing tells*. Many people don't pay attention, or are caught up in their own thoughts.

- *Noticing tells, but not adjusting to them.* Sometimes customer service people notice the cues, but don't have the motivation or skills to adjust their behavior.
- *Noticing tells, but still treating customers as if they have a personality similar to yours.* A customer service representative might see tells accurately and want to adapt, but then might choose the wrong approach. In Jovita's situation, the desk employee might have thought, "She looks kind of down. I'm going to try to get her to lighten up." This hypothetical employee might have had good intentions, but she was most probably doing what she enjoyed and was good at, instead of seeing what Jovita was looking for and satisfying that need.

So we see that, while reading tells is the essential first step, there is also an equally important set of skills we call *responding to tells.*

THREE TYPES OF RESPONSES

You have three options regarding how to act after you notice a tell, and the situation determines which is your best choice. Sometimes you can quickly change your approach based on your observations. Sometimes it makes sense to "say what you see" and tell the customer what you have noticed. And sometimes it's too late to adapt; saying what you see only makes things worse. In these circumstances, learning for the future (about yourself, this customer, or customers in general) may be the bigger payoff.

To repeat, the three responses you can have to customer tells are:

1. Quickly adjust.
2. Say what you see.
3. Learn for the future.

Quickly Adjust

If you scan the list of customer reactions, you will notice that in quite a few cases, the best way to respond to a tell is to say nothing and quickly adjust your behavior. It wouldn't make sense to say, "I notice you're seeking attention, so I will focus on you," or "Your pupils just got larger, so I'm going to keep talking about this option."

If you notice tells indicating boredom or lack of interest, you probably will want to adjust your pace or focus on a different subject, rather than saying, "I see that I'm boring you."

Say What You See

In some customer service interactions, if you don't address your customer's reactions or gather more information, it doesn't make much sense to proceed. For example, if the customer is confused, guarded, or surprised, you may want to say what you see and learn more before you proceed.

You might say something like the following:

- I explain this ten times a day. I realize this is the first time you are hearing about these conditions. I sense I might be going too fast. Would it be better to address one issue at a time? I'll answer all your questions before we move on to the next issue.
- You seem a little hesitant to answer these questions. Are there any concerns you have about the questions or the process?
- It looks as if what I just explained surprised you a little bit. Is this new information, or different from what you were expecting?

Learn for the Future

We all make mistakes. There's no way to predict a customer's personal or cultural sensitivities in every customer service interaction. Eventually we do or say the wrong thing or take the wrong approach. Saying what you see may make the situation more uncomfortable, and perhaps it's too late to improve things by adapting your behavior. The third option is to learn. As the saying goes, "You paid for the lesson already; you might as well take the learning." On the surface this option doesn't seem as satisfying, but in the long run, it can be the most valuable.

When you have time to reflect, analyze the encounter.

- What can you learn about yourself, your impact on people, your behavioral habits, and the skills on which you need to improve?
- What can you learn about the process that will improve it?
- Did you learn about a particular customer's sensitivities?
- Did you learn about a type of customer or customers from a certain culture?

All Three Options

Some reactions, such as anger or frustration, might lead you to choose all three options at different times. Sometimes it's pretty clear why a customer is frustrated, and you simply start using your vocabulary and listening skills to defuse his or her emotions. Other times it may be better to say what you see, demonstrate empathy, and learn the cause of the frustration. Occasionally there is little chance of changing the situation—you can only hope to improve in the future.

With practice and repetition, you will develop a sense of the best option in a particular situation. You won't always get it exactly right, but by reading tells quickly and accurately, you increase your odds of success.

RESPONDING TO KEY CUSTOMER REACTIONS

Now that you understand your three options for responding to tells, let's apply this knowledge to the customer reactions we are most likely to encounter. Here are some suggestions for how to handle each of the customer reactions described in Chapter 7.

1. Interest

The tells indicating a customer is interested in what you are saying are your green light to continue to focus on a subject or, at times, even to go deeper with it. The response is usually to adjust smoothly. If you say what you see—for example, "You just perked up when I talked about delivery time,"—the customer may feel self-conscious, which doesn't help the interaction.

Here is an example of a good use of the quick adjustment response: Kate is a customer service representative for a real estate company that exchanges time-share ownership vacations. She has been talking to two clients, Roberto and Linda, discussing the options and conditions of owning a time-share week and exchanging it for a vacation week in another part of the world.

Linda has been relatively attentive, but Roberto hasn't made much eye contact; mostly he is looking at brochures. Because Linda is paying attention, Kate decides to proceed with the explanation. When she gets to the option of "banking" vacation weeks for future use, she notices that Roberto puts down his brochure and starts making eye contact with her. Based on these tells, she decides to explain the banking option in more detail; she gives Roberto and Linda two examples of how families have used it. Then she asks them some open-ended questions about how predictable their vacation plans are year-to-year. As she suspects, Linda and Roberto can't always plan for definite dates, and they were unaware of the banking option. Working with them, she develops a plan that meets their needs.

In addition to quickly adjusting, the other response that may sometimes apply is learning for the future. It's always useful to learn from success. If a certain way you are phrasing a statement or question seems to be getting customers' attention, or if more and more customers seem interested in a particular aspect of your product or service, this is worth noting for future interactions.

2. Lack of Interest

If you see these tells again, the best approach is usually to adjust quickly. It rarely helps the situation if you say what you see, for example, "It looks like I'm putting you to sleep."

Here is a positive example: Jack works for a firm that provides security to large office buildings. A part of his role is to explain the terms of the service agreements to the operations director at each of the buildings his company works with. Most of the time, these operations directors are thorough and detailed; they expect Jack to go through all aspects of the agreement. Today he is presenting the agreement conditions to a new client, and speaking to operations director Anne and her assistant Jaya.

Jack begins his presentation the way he usually does, but while he is speaking, he notices these tells: Anne and Jaya are both looking at him with blank expressions. They are only nodding occasionally. They aren't asking any questions. Jaya is sitting with his elbow on the table, propping up his chin with his hand.

Jack decides to try a different approach.

Jack: "The rest of the agreement is pretty standard. Can I assume you're familiar with these agreements?"

Anne: "I've probably seen enough of them for one lifetime."

Jack: "Great. There are just two items I need to discuss, for legal reasons. Then we can finish. Please feel free to review the rest of it at your convenience and let me know if you have any questions."

3. Impatience

This is the third reaction that calls for a quick adjustment response. The ability to *match the pace* of your customer is a fundamental skill. If you proceed too fast for your customer, he or she will feel pressured or overwhelmed. If you speak and move more slowly than your customer, you will see the tells of impatience. The most effective response is to adjust your pace without pointing out what you are noticing.

Here is a positive example: Mia is the hostess at an expensive French restaurant in New York City. A regular customer enters the restaurant at 6:50 PM, and inquires about his 7 PM dinner reservation. Mia notices that he doesn't make his usual small talk with her about her studies, his business, or the weather. When she tells him that his table will be ready at 7:00 but isn't available yet, his face shows disappointment. She starts to explain, but he interrupts her and tells her to let him know when it's ready. Mia notices that he sits down and begins drumming his fingers on the chair and tapping his feet on the floor. She goes to the head waiter and gives him these instructions: "Mr. Rodman is here early and seems to be in a hurry. Could you get table seven ready ASAP? Also, tell his server that he may not want to hear all the specials. He may already know what he wants. Ask her to go to his table soon after he arrives, and be prepared to take his food and drink order at the same time."

Mia goes back to Mr. Rodman, walking at a crisp pace, and informs him that the table will be ready earlier than 7:00, and that she will send a server to his table soon after he is seated. Mr. Rodman says, "Thanks, I appreciate it," and smiles for the first time that evening.

4. Something Unexpected

Most often when you observe tells indicating surprise, you know only that the customer is surprised—not necessarily what he is surprised about. Because you remain in the dark about some key information, it makes little sense to keep going, but a lot of sense to say what you see. Comments such as the following can be very useful.

- Is this something different than you were expecting?
- You seem surprised by these conditions.
- Is this new information?
- From your reaction, it looks like this is the first time anyone has brought this to your attention.

What you are trying to learn is what surprised your customer—what was he or she expecting? Even more important, how does the customer feel about this new information?

- Is the customer disappointed? Upset that no one mentioned it before?
- Has the customer lost some trust?
- Has this new information changed the customer's priorities or influenced his or her decision making?
- What have you learned about what is important to this customer?

After you say what you see, use open-ended questions and listening skills to gather information, and then adjust accordingly.

5. Anger

We are confident that you were familiar with some of the tells indicating anger or frustration before you picked up this book. We hope that now, with the list of these tells above, and the discussion of limbic behavior in Chapter 5, you will recognize this reaction quickly. While we don't look forward to these signs, it's inevitable that we see them. Customers sometimes show up upset, or we unintentionally say or do something to trigger their anger.

In some situations you want to adjust quickly and use some of the Golden Rule Fundamental listening skills to learn about the issues at hand and demonstrate empathy; use good vocabulary to reduce and resolve conflict; and use helpful self-talk so that the customer's behavior doesn't push your buttons.

Sometimes there is no opportunity to say what you see, or even to adjust, but there can be great long-term value in learning for the future.

Here is an actual example from Marty's executive coaching practice, where the learning for the future response paid dividends for ten years. Marty received a call from a human resources executive at the international division of his biggest client. "Hi Marty, this is Fred," the executive began. "I'm now the senior vice president of HR for the division. I've replaced Mike, who I understand had you coach some of our executives. We've got someone, James, and I want to send him through your program."

Marty went through the usual process to learn about the issues and objectives of the assignment. When he was finished, he asked a question that was standard in his previous conversations with Fred's predecessor: "Fred, do you want me to talk with James about his next role?"

Almost instantly Marty realized he shouldn't have asked that question. Fred's voice bristled as he shot back loudly, "No, that's my job. That's not your job."

The conversation was all but over, and it was too late to adjust. If Marty had applied the say what you see rule and said, for example, "So, Fred, it sounds like I just made you angry," it would have compounded the original mistake.

The smartest thing for Marty to do was to indicate he got the message, but more importantly, for him to learn something very significant about this potentially key relationship. Even though the tell took five seconds, it gave Marty insight into Fred's strong sense of boundaries. He confirmed this fact with other people who worked with Fred, and kept it in mind when working with him in future. The result was that Fred eventually became the most powerful HR executive at the company, and he remained Marty's client until he retired. In addition, Marty coached several people who worked for Fred, and they always appreciated the heads-up about his strong sense of role clarity.

Just as good poker players have excellent memories for tells and players and can use this information in the future, you also can learn for the future; sometimes this is your most appropriate response.

6. Embarrassment

Here is another reaction that we all try to avoid provoking, but one we may unintentionally trigger. The reason is that for many of us our customer base is incredibly diverse. They arrive with different cultural norms and taboos—for example, they may have different ideas as to the appropriate amount of eye contact, touching, personal space, calling attention to someone's appearance, or formality. They may have different senses of humor, and sensitivities we may not be aware of. This is why, in our customer service role, we may say or do something that causes embarrassment.

Most likely, your preferred response in this situation is to learn for the future, so you can be more sensitive going forward. The incident may expand your awareness of a particular culture, or give you insight into some of your own patterns. Once in a while, in addition to filing away the information for the future, it may be appropriate to apologize.

Here is an example of an embarrassed reaction and an appropriate response: Justin worked in an electronics store that relied on a mostly self-service format. There were no salespeople per se; people like Justin were placed in the customer service role to answer customer questions and be informative. Justin had spent his whole life in the United States, and he wasn't very aware of cultural differences. He tended to be friendly and informal with everyone he met. One day, a husband and wife came into the store to look at a plasma TV. Originally from a Middle Eastern country, they had been in the United States for two years.

Justin's intentions were good, but he missed some important tells early on in the interaction. He should have noticed that the woman was quiet, and talked only to her husband in a soft voice. She was deferential, and avoided eye contact with Justin. His goal, however, was to treat her like an equal partner in the buying decision. He tried to make contact with her and bring her into the discussion. She was showing signs of discomfort already; when he looked at her and asked her directly for her opinion, she withdrew further still.

That tell, and some anger tells from her husband, convinced Justin to adjust. From then on, he talked only to the husband. He also learned some important lessons for the future; he learned about culture, and he learned not to assume that everyone shared his value system.

7. Tentative

When a customer is having difficulty making a decision, it presents a dilemma for a customer service or sales employee. The customer who stays in that state may leave without buying your product or service, greatly reducing the chances he or she will say yes to you in the future. Alternatively, if we don't realize when customers have serious concerns about a decision, we may push too hard and alienate them with our pressure tactics. The best response is often to say what you see, so that you can obtain more information to guide your behavior.

Here is an example: Suzanne is a specialist in the customization and installation of training programs. She works for a small company based in Minneapolis that has a very good reputation. Right now she is working on-site at a client's company. Her manager has told her that this client, Theresa, has agreed to roll out one of their leadership seminars. As Suzanne is discussing the implementation process, she notices that Theresa is exhibiting signs of indecision—she seems reluctant to commit to going forward. She is stroking her chin, using qualifying phrases, and going back and forth on alternatives. Because Suzanne is not sure of the source of Theresa's indecision, she decides to say what she sees.

Suzanne: "You seem a little hesitant to take the next step. Are there any remaining issues on your mind?"

After a pause, Theresa explains that while she's confident Suzanne's company will do a good job, the safer choice for her would be to go with a nationally known and respected training company. "If something goes wrong," she says, "I can never be blamed for going with a nationally recognized company."

Suzanne: "Thanks for being candid with me. What I would like to do is talk with my supervisor and perhaps we can come up with a design for a pilot instead of a full rollout. We are confident it will be well received. Maybe you can have one or two other people from the department attend the pilot and, with luck, reinforce your decision."

8. Anxious

When a customer displays these feelings, unless a longer-term relationship exists, we can't fully know if he or she is nervous about something happening now, or about something entirely unrelated. Unless you know the customer very well, saying what you see might make him or her more self-conscious. Quickly adjusting is your best option. If you think that you, or what you are discussing, is causing the nervousness, you may want to initiate a break. If you are talking to a couple or two friends, give them some space to talk alone. If you are talking with one person, invite him or her to browse alone and talk with you later.

If you think that your presence can be a positive influence, make a sincere effort to project friendliness and warmth through your voice and facial expression. Moods are contagious, and the customer may calm down by picking up on yours.

9. Not Clear

You could be explaining something to a customer and she doesn't really understand what you are saying. You may notice that her eyes glaze over, she stares at a fixed spot, and her pupils do not dilate. She doesn't exhibit normal, timely reactions, and she asks no questions. If you are fortunate, the customer just says, "I'm not following you," "You've lost me," or "You need to say that again, more slowly." Quite often, however, people are embarrassed or otherwise reluctant to admit they are confused. If you see tells indicating confusion but your customer does not say she is puzzled, continuing to talk will only make things worse. The best approach is usually to adjust quickly by using "checking" questions, such as the following:

- I've been giving you a lot of information. Let me stop here. Do you have any questions, or is anything unclear?
- Before I move on to the next item, any reactions to what I've said so far?
- I've been speaking a lot. Let me stop and ask if this is the type of information you are looking for.
- I talk about this 20 times a day, every day. Sometimes I forget people are hearing this for the first time. Let me back up a little; did I cover too much? Any questions?

10. Distrustful/Guarded

Customers are sometimes unsure about the true motives of consultants, salespeople, and customer service people representing the company. As a result, it's not unusual to encounter guarded behavior—for example, closed body language, skeptical questions, sarcastic comments, and hesitant speech patterns. Sometimes you can adjust your behavior and emphasize the customer's self-interest, but often, as in the example below, saying what you see is the best option when you are unsure what is causing the distrust.

Deirdre was recently hired as the vice president in charge of supply chain management at a manufacturing company. She came to this company from a competitor, where her role involved consolidating four plants into two facilities. After a month in her new role, she brought in a consultant, Carlos, with whom she'd worked before. Deirdre had been hired with a mandate to expand the supply chain department, but first she wanted Carlos to interview her team, in order to understand each person's role and responsibilities.

When Carlos interviewed Astrid, he noticed that even though he thought he was asking general, open-ended, nonthreatening questions, she was exhibiting guarded behavior. She would start to speak, then hesitate, and eventually give very vague answers. Carlos decided to stop and say what he saw because the interview was producing very little useful information. He said, "You seem uncomfortable answering some of these questions. If you have any concerns about me or the process, I'd like the opportunity to address them."

Astrid sighed, and finally said, "I've heard rumors that Deirdre was brought in here to consolidate our department, just like she did at her old company."

Carlos immediately saw why Astrid was reluctant to discuss her role. He thanked her and showed her a memo Deirdre had sent to him. It indicated that in fact, Deirdre's objective was to expand. Astrid relaxed, and Carlos was able to conduct a fruitful interview.

11. Seeking Attention

For some people, the attention of others is not simply nice to have—they *need* to have it. Fortunately, the tells for this need are hard to miss, as the discussion of this topic in Chapter 7 indicates. The effective response here is to adjust quickly and meet the customer's need. If you will be interacting with this customer again, remember this attribute. Saying what you see is almost never a good option, because the customer may take it as judgment or criticism. It's helpful here to remind yourself that these kinds of customers are going to be more interested in your product or service after you show an interest in them. You're not wasting time when you do the following:

- Compliment them on some unusual clothing or jewelry.
- Ask questions about their relationship with a famous person they know (name-dropping).
- Show you are impressed with their accomplishments.
- Laugh at their jokes.

12. Happy/Excited

These tells give you feedback on how your product or service connects with your customer. They also may indicate how he or she feels about working with you. Sometimes, when things go well, we celebrate and relax. These are normal reactions, but success is also a great opportunity to learn for the future. Tells of happiness and excitement indicate that you are being successful. It's useful to understand why, so you can replicate that success.

Some good questions to ask yourself or the customer include the following:

- Why is this positive for this customer?
- What does it reveal about the customer's priorities, needs, or core values?
- What feature of our product or service is most important to this customer? (Maybe you should emphasize this feature more when dealing with other customers.)
- What did I do right that I might want to do again?
- Is there any knowledge here that would interest my supervisors?

10

COMMUNICATION STYLE HABITS

In the next six chapters you will learn about the second key category of tells: communication style tells. While in-the-moment tells indicate how the customer is reacting right now, communication style tells indicate a deep-seated habit or pattern of behavior. Poker professionals rely on both of these types of tells. They will observe in-the-moment tells to gather information about how an opponent is playing this hand. At the same time they look for signals about the overall playing styles of their opponents. For example, playing styles can vary among tight/passive, loose/passive, loose/aggressive, and tight/aggressive. We realize that these categories won't mean too much to you unless you are a poker player, but we wanted to illustrate that in poker, as in customer service, we are often interacting with people who display clear patterns of behavior.

This ability to detect patterns or styles potentially yields even more information than in-the-moment tells. It can open a whole new world of information about our key goal: How does this customer want to be treated? We are creatures of habit and that makes each of us more predictable than we realize. Before we discuss the four main types of communication styles we need to learn more about habits—communication habits.

As human beings, we have more capacity than any other species to become aware of our habits and change them. As the microbiologist and environmentalist Rene Dubos said about human behavior, "Trend is not destiny." In other words, we all have the potential to make remarkable changes. We tend, however, to repeat habits and patterns. Thus the saying: "Human beings are creatures of habit," making us much more predictable than we realize.

Behavioral psychologists estimate that habits make up 80 to 90 percent of our behavior. Think about driving to work. Do you take the same route? Does it annoy you when construction forces a detour? Do you ever drive to work, and once you get there, you don't really remember the journey? It's as if you were on autopilot or going through the motions without really thinking. If you answered yes, you are not alone. Waking up, eating breakfast, and brushing your teeth are often habitual actions—you do the same thing day after day. Interestingly, when engaging in habitual behavior we are much less likely to be conscious of what we are doing. In fact, we are conscious of our habits only about 40 percent of the time.

Shouldn't we be thinking more about what we're doing? Not necessarily. Our unconscious actions fit a defining characteristic of habits—their efficiency. Habits allow us to perform tasks without feeling burdened, overworked, or overwhelmed. Conscious behavior requires thought and decision making, increasing the time and energy we expend. When learning to ride a bicycle, for example, we can do little else but concentrate on staying upright. However, once we have mastered it, we can ride without thinking much about it. People develop standard patterns of response that reduce the amount of thought required for actions.

However, people may use an established behavior pattern even when it's no longer the most effective response or the response that they intend to give, according to Texas A&M University psychologist Wendy Wood. Habits are cued by the environment, and when the appropriate cues are present they may emerge even if they're not appropriate. Habits are efficient, but that doesn't mean they are optimal in every situation. And this is certainly true for your communication habits. In Chapter 14 we will give you several examples of the potential limitation of always staying within your communication habits.

To fully appreciate the impact of habits, it's important to understand not only their prevalence in our behavior (80 to 90 percent) but also their power of dictating our behavior. To accomplish this we will ask you to complete a basic exercise. Lean back, relax, and fold your arms against your chest. Now let your arms fall to your sides. This time, fold your arms again, but switch their positions: put the top arm on the bottom, and vice versa. It probably feels awkward and somehow wrong. Perhaps you had to think about it before you did it, and maybe you're not sure if you actually did it differently at all. You never thought about it before, because you'd done it so many times. The way we fold our arms is a habit, and as with all other habits; it's a groove, or an established pattern in our nervous system and therefore holds great power.

As our brain develops, it creates "shortcuts" that bypass certain decision making processes when we encounter familiar stimuli or execute familiar actions, such as crossing our arms. So, our brain "does the thinking for us" when we cross our arms, but when we try something new—for example, if we are learning to swing a golf club—we have to think through the actions, concentrate, and actively "tell our body" what to do in order to hit the golf ball. Therefore, our habits are very persistent, unless we bring a high level of awareness and intention to changing them. We speak more about the importance of this concept a little later.

In the paragraphs above we have been discussing the nature of our habits in general. The focus of the Communication Styles Model is the area of communication habits. Examples of communication habits include hand gestures, pace of speech, speed of decision making, choice of words, and listening. Naturally, the same rules of habits apply to communication habits as well—they are very prevalent (80 to 90 percent of all communication is governed by our habits) and very powerful, meaning that they also fall into the category of consistent and predictable. The purpose of the Communication Styles Model is to leverage this reality by becoming astute at reading communication habits and then adapting our behavior to facilitate the best possible interaction. The Communication Styles Model is the product of organizing communication style habits along two dimensions. We discuss the dimensions, and how to analyze communication habits and organize the information to discover the customer's communication style in great detail in the next several chapters.

In addition to becoming experts on reading other's communication habits (and, as a result their communication style), we also need to become experts on our communication habits to ensure we are adapting successfully. Why is it so crucial to be keenly aware of our own habits? Let's take a moment for some self-reflection before you answer this question. Have you ever been engaged in a conversation with someone and you clearly had good intentions, perhaps you were trying to help him or her solve a problem or to offer good advice, yet, somewhere along the way the other person appeared to shut down or was frustrated and ended the conversation in a negative way? You may have been left wondering, "What happened; I was only trying to help?"

Many times, this type of outcome is the result of a lack of awareness of a communication habit. Perhaps it was your tone of voice, your choice of words, or simply your facial expression that caused the negative outcome. Meaning, a lack of awareness of communication habits may frequently undermine your best efforts when interacting with a customer. This is why it's so important to be as aware as you can be of your interpersonal habits. If you are aware of your habits, you can choose your behavior consciously to minimize these kinds of inadvertent mishaps and ensure that your intention meets your impact.

As it turns out, in the area of communication habits, self-awareness has a unique challenge: It's the one area of your life where other people get more information on you than you get on yourself! The simple reason for this is that we very rarely observe ourselves from the outside when we are interacting with others. In fact, we rarely observe ourselves from the outside at all. For most of us it's only when looking in the mirror while getting ready to leave the house that we observe ourselves. As a result, we actually get very little information on our communication habits. Conversely, those who spend a lot of time with you—family, friends, or coworkers who have observed you thousands of times when you are interacting with others—have extensive information on your communication habits. For example, in 2001, Marty and his wife, Kelly, adopted a three-year-old girl, Jyoti, from Gujarat, India. She didn't speak English, but was eager to learn. About two months after her arrival she had picked up some English words. One day in their living room, she started to make certain facial expressions and hand movements. Kelly started giggling, but Marty was mystified.

Marty: "What is she doing and what is so funny?"

Kelly: "Jyoti is imitating you."

Marty: "I don't do that!"

Kelly: "That's exactly what you do."

Then Kelly and Jyoti laughed even harder. Jyoti's powers of observation were not unique, although they may have been sharper in new surroundings. Marty's unawareness of his own habits is common to all of us.

When we watch ourselves on videotape, we often find ourselves saying things like, "Is that what I do?" or "I don't look like that, do I?" The camera frequently catches us doing things of which we may be completely unaware. Ben recently saw himself on tape using the same hand gesture over and over again—he felt he looked ridiculous, and he had no idea that he was making the gesture so repetitively. Seeing and hearing yourself on video is often awkward—all your unconscious physical and verbal habits are suddenly glaringly apparent.

So, while we are the experts on our insides—our intentions, dreams, hopes, and fears—other people are probably the experts on our outsides. Considering how important it is for excellent communication, our goal in the next few chapters is help you close this gap, to have you become an expert on your outsides or communication habits. Throughout our discussion of the Communications Style Model we will continuously ask you to reflect on your own habits. Also, in Chapters 11 and 12 we dedicated sections specifically to the process of recognizing your own style. After you have determined your style, Chapter 15 addresses in detail the potential challenges you will face with the other three styles.

11

DIMENSIONS OF THE COMMUNICATION STYLES MODEL

Now that we have established the prevalence, power, and predictability of styles tells, we need the ability to read and categorize them accurately. The Communication Styles Model provides you with the tool to understand and assess the different styles tells. The model is composed of two style dimensions: *directness* and *relationship building*. This chapter offers an in-depth understanding of the two dimensions, and will teach you to read and categorize the various style tells along the appropriate dimension. This combination of insight and skill forms the foundation of the Communication Styles Model.

THE TWO DIMENSIONS

Each of the dimensions of the Communications Style Model divides individuals into two categories. The directness dimension is divided into direct and indirect approaches of communicating, while the relationship building dimension is split between those focused more on people and those focused more toward tasks. In order to determine where a customer lies on either dimension, we need to consider six different style tell clusters specific to the dimension. Use of the six clusters helps us to avoid making a decision based on too little information. In the following section, we describe the six clusters for directness and indirectness, and explain how to determine a customer's place on this dimension.

THE DIMENSION OF DIRECTNESS

The six tell clusters that determine a customer's level of directness are: voice volume, pace, conviction, decision making, communication, and posture. Your reading of these clusters lets you determine where your customer falls on the directness scale.

The Direct Individual

Direct individuals tend to exhibit the following six behaviors:

1. *High volume.* Direct people have a louder voice and a more assertive tone than indirect people. They're often easy to spot, because you can hear them from across the room. You rarely have to ask them to repeat themselves. Whether you talk to them in person or on the phone, it will be easy to pick up on the volume of their voice.
2. *Fast pace.* These customers talk and act fast; patience is not their greatest virtue. They may walk ahead of you as you are showing them a product. They also tend to interrupt more.
3. *Strong conviction.* These individuals speak with great conviction; they use words and phrases that convey certainty, such as *clearly, obviously,* or "This is a no-brainer." They will rarely use qualifying words and phrases such as *maybe, perhaps,* or "One idea might be…" It is important to note that this pattern of speech doesn't necessarily mean they are correct; they may just sound as if they are.

4. *Faster decisions.* Direct customers often make decisions quickly. They don't feel the need to study the options for too long—instead, they take the information presented to them and determine a course of action fairly quickly.

5. *Demanding, not asking.* Direct people are comfortable telling you what they think you should do. They often don't feel the need to ask politely or to ask you what might be easiest or your preference. They use phrases such as "you have to," "you should," or "you must." They might imply, or even state, that they know more about your business than you do. Direct customers are not afraid of confrontation, and (as you may have experienced) do not shy away from it. Additionally, many are not expert diplomats; they often make stronger statements than are necessary, such as "What idiots came up with that policy?" when a phrase like, "I have some questions about the policy," would have been more tactful.

6. *Upright posture.* Direct customers are more upright in their posture and often lean forward slightly when talking.

The Indirect Individual

Indirect individuals often exhibit the following six behaviors:

1. *Low volume.* Indirect people tend to be soft-spoken. You may find it hard to hear them, and may need to ask them to repeat themselves.

2. *Slow pace.* Indirect customers tend to speak more slowly and pause longer between words. They also may become quiet, or need time to reflect on what is being discussed.

3. *Less conviction.* Indirect customers' style of speech is more tentative. They use qualifiers such as *I might, perhaps,* or *maybe* before making a statement.

4. *Slower to decide.* Indirect people prefer to take more time to make a decision. They like to gather as much data as

possible and explore all available options beforehand. This is the kind of customer who will ask a hotel employee to describe all the available rooms, and compare summer rates to off-season prices.

5. *More asking/listening.* Indirect people are more comfortable asking rather than telling. They use phrases such as "Would it be possible," "Would it be too much trouble," or "Would you mind," when making requests. Uncomfortable with conflict, they avoid it if possible, but they may express frustration or disappointment by not returning to the business. Additionally, indirect individuals are more patient, which can make them more skillful and polite listeners than direct customers.

6. *Laid-back posture.* The indirect customer is more laid back than the direct customer, not as likely to lean forward when in discussion, and also unlikely to get too close to you when talking.

Except for the posture tell, a customer can easily display the others over the phone. Marty maintained positive phone relationships with some of his clients for seven years before ever meeting them in person. During those years, he used their phone tells as a guidance system:

Phone Tells

	Indirect Customer	Direct Customer
Volume	Softer	Louder
Pace	Slower	Quicker
Conviction	Less	More
Decisiveness	Takes time to weigh the options, often pauses on the phone	Fast decision maker
Demanding/ Listening	More listening	More demanding or requesting

Self-Evaluation

Now that we have described direct and indirect customers, we would like you to evaluate where *you* fall on this dimension. As you consider where you would place yourself on each of the six behavior clusters we ask you to focus on your behavior *while you are working.* Some people display similar communication habits regardless of the situation they're in. Others operate one way at work, another way at home with their family, and still another way at happy hour!

You probably have exhibited behaviors from both sides of the directness dimension; almost all of us display a range of behavior. Remember, though, that our habits are often more consistent than we realize. This exercise attempts to determine your comfort zone, the type of behavior you feel most comfortable with, and that you most often display at work. Start off with the volume of your speech: Do you generally have a softer voice or are you louder? Check the corresponding box in Figure 11.1. Then do the same for the rest of the behaviors. Remember, there is no right or wrong way of being—everybody has the right to his or her own style. The key is to be self-aware and to be able to adapt your style so that you can communicate effectively with anyone.

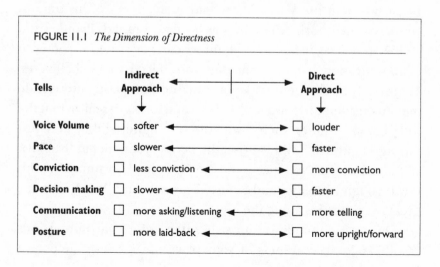

FIGURE 11.1 *The Dimension of Directness*

Predictable Issues of Differences in Directness

Directness and indirectness are equally valid styles; one is not better than the other. However, differences in approach often lead to misperception and misunderstanding. For example, differing paces of speech can create mutual frustration. The direct and faster-paced individual may become aggravated with people who speak more slowly and elaborately. "Get to the point," or "Just give it to me in bullets," such a person may think, or perhaps even say out loud. Likewise, someone who speaks quickly and interrupts might frustrate the indirect, slower-paced individual, who needs time to process information and think things through. The direct person's fast decision-making, assertive, and demanding language, and poor listening skills may make the indirect person think of the direct one as rude, reckless, confrontational, or arrogant.

The indirect person's tendency toward slower decision making and use of tentative language may result in being seen by direct people as slow, indecisive, weak, or lacking confidence. John first started working with Marty more than nine years ago. John had spent most of his life in northern Florida, where people are generally more indirect. There, politeness, patience, and listening are paramount when communicating with others. When John began working for Marty, Marty had spent much of his time in Brooklyn, New York, where he was born and raised. People from Brooklyn generally fall into the direct category when it comes to communication habits. John, therefore, faced some challenges. He initially made the mistake of thinking that people were rude and inconsiderate. It also took him several weeks to realize that the folks hanging out on their stoop were not fighting; they were just having a conversation! Likewise, the people John met in Brooklyn perceived him as "too nice," and "wishy-washy." Fortunately, John saw through his biases and adjusted his behavior, building many great relationships along the way.

Our own communication style often colors our impressions of others. Your awareness of your place on this scale helps you understand how you may be perceived by someone who operates differently, and show you how to adapt your style to avoid these negative customer reactions.

THE DIMENSION OF RELATIONSHIP BUILDING

The second dimension of the Communication Styles Model is relationship building. Just as the dimension of directness has a direct versus indirect scale, relationship building has a *task-focus* versus a *relationship-focus* scale. The relationship dimension is signaled by six behavior clusters: approach, facial expressions, body and hands, work orientation, decision making, and vocal inflection. Your reading of these clusters lets you determine where your customer falls on the scale.

Task Focus

Task-focused people exhibit the following six behaviors:

1. *Serious approach.* Task-focused customers tend not to smile as much, and may have stern facial expressions. They rarely make jokes—be prepared for them not to laugh at your attempts to get them to lighten up.
2. *Fewer facial expressions.* Task-focused individuals have fewer facial expressions—they have natural poker faces. They can be difficult to read; it's hard to know whether they are happy, excited, or upset. They are more emotionally controlled, appearing cool and calm much of the time.
3. *Set body and hands.* These customers move their hands less when they talk, making them appear formal and professional.
4. *Work orientation.* These customers focus on what they need to achieve—whether making travel arrangements or asking

for help. They may avoid small talk or icebreakers, moving directly to the task at hand.

5. *Logic.* These customers base decisions on objective, rational thought and fact. They ask for specific prices, contract terms, and other details. The task-focused customer rarely makes a gut decision.

6. *Less vocal inflection.* In congruence with their cool, calm, and collected way of interaction, task-focused individuals have a more monotone manner of speaking. You rarely hear dramatic inflections in their vocal patterns.

Relationship-Focus

People who are relationship-focused exhibit the following six attributes:

1. *Fun-loving approach.* Relationship-focused customers often believe, "We only live once, so let's have fun while we're here." Even when they're in the customer role, they are usually smiling, joking, and trying to bring levity and laughter into the interaction.

2. *More facial expressions.* Sunglasses won't help these folks too much with their poker faces; they might have to wear a Halloween mask. Whether coworker, friend or customer, we rarely have to ask them how they are feeling—it's usually written all over their faces.

3. *Mobile body and hands.* Relationship-focused customers' hands are a more integral part of how they communicate. We've all seen people gesticulating while on the phone. Their phone partner obviously can't see them, but they can't really express themselves without using their hands.

4. *People orientation.* While relationship-focused people still have a goal to accomplish in a customer service interaction, their relationship with you, the customer service professional, is very important to them. If they feel a personal

bond, they're more likely to have a positive interaction. Often more talkative, they attempt to bond with you by sharing personal information or asking you questions.

5. *Intuitive.* Relationship-focused individuals don't abandon facts and logic; however, they are much more likely to factor in feelings and intuition when making decisions. You may hear them say, "This just doesn't feel right," or "The price seems right, but there is something I just can't put my finger on...."

6. *More vocal inflection.* Just as relationship-focused customers display animated body language, hand gestures, and speech, so too the volume and tone of their speech communicate their feelings more dramatically than task-focused people.

Phone Tells		
	Task-Focused Customer	**Relationship-Focused Customer**
Approach	Serious, not as likely to joke	Fun-loving
Work Orientation	Focused on accomplishing the tasks at hand, unlikely to share personal information	Will ask "how are you" or share personal stories
Conviction	Uses qualifiers such as "maybe" or "this is what I am leaning towards"	Might say "I need" or "This is what I want"
Vocal Inflection	Speaks mostly in monotone	Likely to convey a sense of surprise, excitement, or frustration through pitch

Self-Evaluation

Now, just as you did with the directness scale, evaluate where you fall on the dimension of relationship building in Figure 11.2. Again, while your behavior varies from situation to situation, you should focus on your comfort zone in the workplace.

Predictable Issues of Relationship-Building Differences

As with the directness dimension, differences between the task-focused person and the relationship-focused person can lead to misunderstandings—in fact, in our experience differences in this dimension create more conflict than in the directness scale.

The relationship-focused individual may perceive the task-focused person as too serious, uptight, dull, a stick-in-the-mud, boring, too hard to read, or no fun. He or she might see the task-focused person's focus on logic and objectivity as too narrow and close-minded, as if that person "can't see the forest for the trees." Perhaps the task-focused person's greatest difference from the relationship-focused person is a reserved and private nature, and therefore a seeming disinterest in forming personal connections.

FIGURE 11.2 *The Dimension of Relationship Building*

Tells	Approach	Facial Expressions	Body and Hands	Work Orientation	Decision Making	Vocal Inflection
	☐	☐	☐	☐	☐	☐
Task Focus ➤	Serious	Less	Set	Task	Logic	Less
	↕	↕	↕	↕	↕	↕
Relationship Focus ➤	Fun-loving	More	Mobile	People	Intuition	More
	☐	☐	☐	☐	☐	☐

We have often heard relationship-focused people mistake this behavior for rudeness, insensitivity, aloofness, haughtiness, or indifference. They may interpret the lack of conversation and connection as a sign of dislike or a hidden agenda.

Relationship-focused types are equally vulnerable to task-focused customers' negative perceptions. The task-focused person often sees the relationship-focused person as frivolous or unprofessional, and more interested in having fun than doing his job. Task-focused people may find their emotional expressiveness immature and annoying, calling them "drama kings or queens" or "high maintenance." Because task-focused individuals are more private, relationship-focused people's personal chit-chat could strike them as inappropriate, intrusive, and time-wasting. Task-focused people distrust feelings or intuition when it comes to decision making: Because relationship-focused people use these tools often, task-focused folk may think they're not truly objective and are therefore a poor source of advice.

Ben was judged in this manner when he first started working at a large accounting firm in New York City. Ben is largely relationship focused, but a significant number of his fellow team members were task focused. As he walked through the office, he often greeted coworkers with a big "Hello!" and asked how they were doing. He quickly found, however, that many of them were actually startled, taken aback by his enthusiasm, and not overly excited about exchanging pleasantries in the midst of a fast-paced workday. Realizing that his communication habits were possibly alienating him from his teammates—occasionally he noticed coworkers discreetly trying to avoid him in the halls—Ben took his highly enthusiastic style down a notch.

To reiterate, it's no better or worse to be task-focused or relationship focused. It is critical, however, to be aware of your own communication habits and possible misperceptions that could adversely affect your interaction. In the next chapter we discuss how to adapt our behavior and maintain our self-awareness.

You now have an understanding of the two dimensions of communication habits and the styles tells associated with each of them. We hope that we have convinced you of the importance of self-awareness and have begun to discover where you fall on the two dimensions. In the next chapter, we put the two dimensions together to form the Communication Styles Model and look at more tells to help you identify each style.

Chapter

12

FOUR
COMMUNICATION
STYLES

Now that we understand the two dimensions that comprise the Communications Styles Model, we will describe how these dimensions combine to create four distinct communication styles. By picking up styles tells and placing them along the dimensions of directness or relationship building, you can discern a person's style. You will learn characteristics of the four styles and additional tells to help you determine which style best fits the customer with whom you are interacting.

THE COMMUNICATION STYLES MODEL

The Communication Styles Model brings the two dimensions of directness and relationship building together as X and Y axes, as shown in Figure 12.1.

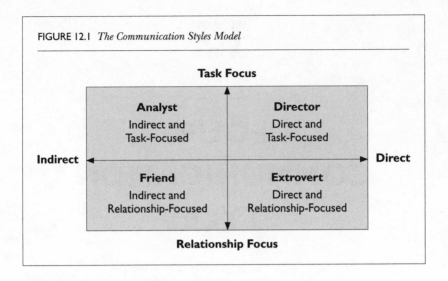

FIGURE 12.1 *The Communication Styles Model*

THE FOUR STYLES

The following are important points to remember before applying the model.

- The purpose of the model is not to pigeonhole or stereotype customers.
- Everyone (including you) has elements of each style; however, most people have a dominant style or comfort zone that they work within most of the time. This is what we are looking for.
- No style is any better or worse than any other. The key is to be aware of our own style and to adapt when the situation requires it.
- The model focuses on an individual's interpersonal behavioral habits. Communication style has no correlation to intelligence, integrity, compassion, or any other quality.
- As with any model, the Communication Styles Model is not a perfect reflection of reality. There are certainly exceptions to these rules, and it's rare that everything about a particular communication style applies to any one person. The model

is simply a guidance mechanism for effectively interacting with others.

As you read the following section, take note of which character attributes you feel fit you best.

Our examination of each communication style includes the following:

- *A general description of the style.* Its traits, its focus, and how people of this style make decisions.
- *The strengths of the style.* Each style tends to have certain natural strengths.
- *The key behavioral tells of the style.* The verbal and nonverbal behaviors typical of the style.
- *A celebrity example.* A celebrity who embodies the characteristics of each style.

THE ANALYST: INDIRECT AND TASK FOCUSED

Analysts are usually cautious and thoughtful. They like to gather as much information and detail as possible before making a decision. To reduce risk and increase accuracy and precision, Analysts like to explore all possible options. They are systematic thinkers and rely on objectivity and logic.

Strengths of Analysts

- Objectivity
- Precision
- Thoroughness, attention to detail
- Systematic thinking
- Professional approach
- Willingness to explore alternatives
- Tendency to encourage others to think carefully, be rational

Tells of Analysts

- Analysts tend to show very little emotion and, as a result, have limited facial expressions. They often have natural poker faces. They don't gesticulate much, often making them appear formal or professional.
- They are usually reserved with softer voices and less vocal inflection.
- They often ask for a lot of details and facts regarding the topic at hand.
- They've probably done their homework and may begin interaction armed with all the data they could find about the topic.
- They tend to speak with precision, choosing their words carefully, and using a slightly slower pace. Sometimes they correct themselves midsentence if they feel they have chosen an inaccurate word.
- They rarely use generalizations or exaggerations such as "Fantastic," "This is the greatest thing since sliced bread," or "This will be a home run."
- They are more likely to ask than tell, and therefore use phrases such as, "Would it be possible," or "One idea I have is," as opposed to "I need you to," or "You must."
- They're more private and task-focused, and therefore rarely make small talk or try to connect personally if they don't know a person well. They likely will focus on their objective right away.

Celebrity Analyst: Bill Gates

The cofounder of Microsoft Corporation known for his detail orientation and thoughtfulness is a classic Analyst. He values precision, especially when it comes to language; in a 1998 deposition testimony, Gates questioned the definitions of specific words as a part of making his case. He likes to accomplish tasks; when his employees struggle to complete programming assignments, he is rumored to joke, "Do you want me to do it over the weekend?" Gates is uncomfortable with the attention his vast wealth brings. He would rather place the spotlight on his business and philanthropic endeavors, not on his money or his personality. As a result he's not often seen on television or in the public eye.

THE DIRECTOR: DIRECT AND TASK-FOCUSED

Directors are fast-paced and decisive, and they can be impatient with those who don't keep up with them. They tend to take action quickly, based on information they consider relevant, and correct their course later if needed. They specialize in pragmatism, candidness, coolness under pressure, and completing tasks quickly.

Strengths of Directors

- Decisiveness
- Toughness
- Efficiency
- Candidness
- Results-orientation
- Pragmatism
- Willingness to take risks
- Tendency to encourage others to decide and take action

Tells of Directors

- Directors' strongest tell is their need to be in control of most situations.

- Directors tend to speak quickly with an assertive tone and at times a loud voice.
- They often make direct and prolonged eye contact when engaging with you.
- Directors tend to speak in a very concise manner, using few words to make their point.
- They use very few qualifiers (such as "maybe," "perhaps," "sort of," or "would it be silly if . . . ") in their speech, instead using language that suggests conviction, such as:
- Clearly...
- Obviously...
- You should...
- Logically...
- What I need is...
- What I'm looking for...
- They make decisions fairly quickly.
- Their body language often is intense and forward leaning.
- Because they are task-focused, they immediately express their needs, and spend little time trying to create a personal connection.
- They are the least patient of the styles and may be more likely to interrupt while you are speaking.

Celebrity Director: Tiger Woods

Tiger Woods has established himself as one of the greatest golfers of all time. He is the career victories leader among active players on the PGA Tour, the career money list leader, and the youngest golfer ever to win 50 PGA Tour tournaments. Woods has focused on achievement and results ever since he began playing golf as a two-year-old at the encouragement of his father, Earl Woods, who taught him discipline, efficiency, and mental toughness. At three, Tiger was already on television, showcasing his prodigious talent. A great performer under pressure, Tiger has said one of his greatest assets is that "I am the toughest golfer mentally." Tiger's singular, results-oriented focus on the golf course is evident in every one of his calculated moves. His assertion, "My main focus is on my game," lets us know he is a true Director. Known for practicing much longer than most other golfers, Tiger is also committed to a strenuous fitness regimen and has been called almost machinelike during tournaments. He nearly always wears a red shirt during the final round of tournaments as he believes the color symbolizes aggression and assertiveness. Showing his Directorial confidence and drive, Tiger admits, "I did envisage being this successful as a player." (Smith, December 23, 1996)

THE FRIEND: INDIRECT AND RELATIONSHIP-FOCUSED

Friends are considerate and supportive. Their demeanor is relaxed and patient. They demonstrate compassion, loyalty, compromise, and trust. Friends take their time making decisions and relationships are often a major factor in their choice. Friends are likely to weigh the pros and cons of a decision based on how it might affect other people.

Strengths of Friends

- Supportiveness
- Empathy
- Trustworthiness
- Loyalty
- Team orientation
- Concern for others' development
- Willingness to share recognition
- Tendency to encourage others to look for win-win solutions

Tells of Friends

- Friends are consistently the most polite of the four communication styles. Expect to hear phrases such as "Thank you," and "Excuse me."
- Friends speak at a slow, relaxed pace.
- Friends have laid-back body language.
- They have pronounced facial expressions, and smile readily.
- Friends enjoy personal connection, and likely will make small talk before getting down to business.
- Friends are patient listeners and rarely interrupt.
- Friends demonstrate empathy and compassion.
- Like Analysts, Friends tend to use qualifying words or phrases.
- Friends generally do not use demanding language, relying instead on indirect phrases such as:
  - Would it be possible…
  - What if we tried…
- Friends are likely to ask personal questions about you, and tell you about themselves.
- Friends are likely to make supportive comments such as "Yes, I agree," or "I feel the same way."

Celebrity Friend: Mr. Rogers

The Reverend Frederick Rogers was an American educator, minister and, from 1968 to 2001, the host of the internationally acclaimed children's television show, *Mister Rogers' Neighborhood*. He went into television because he felt it was a "fabulous instrument to nurture those who would watch and listen." His wish to connect with others is a core Friend quality. Mr. Rogers began each episode singing his theme song, "Won't You Be My Neighbor?" The song's title is an excellent illustration of the Friend's tendency to seek a bond with others through listening and personal storytelling. Rogers's relaxed style was evident when he changed into comfortable clothing at the beginning of every episode, and also when he spoke with guests or visited a local store. Each episode included a trip to the "Neighborhood of Make-Believe," ruled by King Friday XIII. Topics discussed there included helping friends in difficult times, conflict with siblings, and making choices in tough situations. "Everybody longs to be loved," Rogers once said. "The greatest thing we can do is let somebody know that they are loved and capable of loving." Rogers also tried to address common childhood fears with comforting songs and skits, once going to a hospital to show children that it wasn't a place to be afraid of. A tireless advocate for the education and welfare of children, Rogers displayed the Friend's characteristic team orientation, saying, "We live in a world in which we need to share responsibility... [the people who share responsibility are] my heroes." (Rogers, 2001) The Friend's emphasis on personal connection can be contagious: When Rogers's car was stolen, local news channels picked up the story. Within 48 hours, the car was back in the spot where he'd left it, along with a note saying "If we'd known it was yours, we never would have taken it." (Rogers, 1985)

THE EXTROVERT: DIRECT AND RELATIONSHIP-FOCUSED

Extroverts are fast-moving, fast-talking individuals. They like to be original and creative. They have lots of energy, a good sense of humor, and like to take risks. They tend to decide fairly quickly, using their feelings and intuition, often in the process.

Strengths of the Extrovert

- Creativity
- A sense of fun
- Enthusiasm
- Energy
- Focus on the vision

- Team spirit
- Willingness to try new things
- Tendency to encourage others to be the best, break new ground

Tells of Extroverts

- Extroverts tend to talk fast and use lots of vocal inflection.
- Extroverts probably talk the most of all the styles, and can sometimes dominate conversations.
- They use a lot of facial expressions and hand gestures; they wear their emotions on their sleeves.
- They like to inject humor into a conversation, and often make jokes.
- Extroverts tend to be the least formal of the styles, and may call you nicknames like *pal, buddy, champ, darling,* or *sweetheart,* right from your first meeting. Their informality might also include standing closer to you and touching you more.
- Extroverts like being the center of attention, and tend to talk about themselves a lot. They may wear attention-getting clothing or jewelry.
- They speak with enthusiasm and conviction, using phrases such as:
  - Amazing
  - Fantastic
  - Out of this world
  - This is the best ever
- They tend to brag and name-drop more than the other styles.

Celebrity Extrovert: President Bill Clinton

The charismatic 42nd President of the United States is a classic Extrovert. He is an engaging public speaker who is passionate about many philanthropic topics. His facial expressions and hand gestures are famously expressive with comedy shows such as *Saturday Night Live* often lampooned his lip-biting, winking, and use of the thumbs-up gesture. He has a keen sense of humor, and his informal, down-home attitude makes it easy for him to get along with many different types of people. President Clinton often cannot help being the center of attention wherever he goes highlighting the fact that an Extrovert rarely moves out of the spotlight.

IDENTIFYING YOUR OWN COMMUNICATION STYLE

In the previous sections, we discussed the importance of consciously understanding your own communication habits and style in order to prevent inadvertently undermining customer interactions. We provided you with extensive style tells to help you identify others' communication styles; these tells also give you clues as to your own style. We have also asked you to reflect on your own habits. Now you will put all this information together. First, please refer to your assessment of your place on the two dimensions from Chapter 11. This information will help determine your style. Using the model on page 146, where would you place yourself in the communication styles model?

Next, review the information we provided for each of the styles—the general descriptions, strengths, and tells—and decide which of the four styles seems most like you. You might identify with a few different styles—as we explained earlier, we each have aspects of all four styles, but most of us have a dominant style. To find yours, we ask you to complete the final self-assessment exercise in Figure 12.2. Combine all the data you have gathered so far (dimensions and styles data), and insert the numbers 1, 2, 3, or 4 in each of the style boxes (one number per box), with 1 representing what you believe to be your most dominant style, 2 representing your second most dominant style, 3 the third, and 4 in the box that you least identify with. By completing this exercise

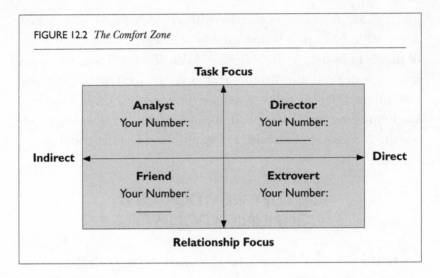

FIGURE 12.2 *The Comfort Zone*

you will have identified your comfort zone (your number 1 style) and gained a more complete picture of your overall style.

The final and most crucial step in accurately assessing your style is receiving feedback. Remember the unique nature of communication habits—while we are the experts on our insides, others are the experts on our outsides. Now is the time to get help from these experts. To ensure that your self-assessment matches the way others perceive you, find a coworker, preferably someone whom you have worked with for a while, and explain to him or her your self-assessment (both the dimensions and the comfort zone exercise). Ask, "Do you agree with my assessment? Is there any area where you see me differently?" It's critical that you don't become defensive if he or she gives you feedback that's different from your self-analysis; remember that this colleague is truly doing you a favor. Realize also that his or her feedback is not right or wrong—it's simply another person's perspective. This coworker's opinion, however, may be representative of most people's perception of you, and therefore very important information. For the best results, choose a minimum of three coworkers to ask for feedback; this way, you will reduce the chance of receiving feedback colored by personal bias.

13

READING COMMUNICATION STYLES

The previous two chapters focused on gaining the insight necessary to effectively apply the Communication Styles Model. In the next three chapters we focus on reading styles and what to do once we recognize them. This chapter concentrates on reading styles. Becoming skilled at reading styles—picking up and organizing the various styles tells—is paramount. If you cannot read styles, you will have limited ability to use the model despite all your current insight.

This chapter includes:

- Utilizing the styles scorecard and the additional styles tells
- Skill practice—applying the process to four celebrities
- A skill practice debrief
- Additional tips on practicing reading styles

THE STYLE SCORECARD AND ADDITIONAL STYLES TELLS

The two-step process of reading a person's style is similar to the method you used to assess you own style. First, we want to find out where a person falls on the two dimensions of directness and relationship building. In order to accomplish this task we need to evaluate him or her according to a styles scorecard, an example of which is shown in Figure 13.1.

Just as it did for your self-assessment, the completion of this scorecard will give you crucial information about a person's

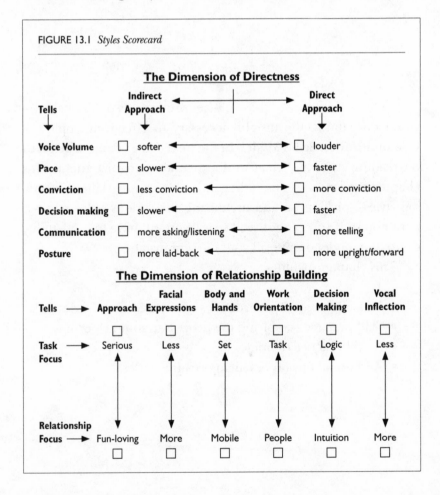

FIGURE 13.1 *Styles Scorecard*

The Dimension of Directness

Tells	Indirect Approach		Direct Approach
Voice Volume	☐ softer	➡	☐ louder
Pace	☐ slower	➡	☐ faster
Conviction	☐ less conviction	➡	☐ more conviction
Decision making	☐ slower	➡	☐ faster
Communication	☐ more asking/listening	➡	☐ more telling
Posture	☐ more laid-back	➡	☐ more upright/forward

The Dimension of Relationship Building

Tells ➡	Approach	Facial Expressions	Body and Hands	Work Orientation	Decision Making	Vocal Inflection
	☐	☐	☐	☐	☐	☐
Task Focus ➡	Serious	Less	Set	Task	Logic	Less
	⬆	⬆	⬆	⬆	⬆	⬆
Relationship Focus ➡	Fun-loving	More	Mobile	People	Intuition	More
	☐	☐	☐	☐	☐	☐

dominant communication style. To ensure thoroughness and to help you with people who are hard to place on the dimensions, we look for tells that are specific to each style.

For example, if we were reading the tells of actor Jim Carrey and trying to decide his dominant style, the styles scorecard would look like the one in Figure 13.2.

Canadian-born Carrey is best known for his wacky comedy films, which have made him one of Hollywood's biggest stars. His outlandish characters include the title character in *Ace Ventura: Pet Detective,* the Riddler in *Batman Forever,* and the Grinch in *How the Grinch Stole Christmas.* While these characters are roles Carrey plays, he infuses them with his personality, providing us with ample information as to where he falls on the dimension of directness. Carrey is not a soft-spoken person, both in character and in real life: he sings, yells, and generally can be heard across the room. He moves fairly quickly, and speaks rapidly and with conviction. He's known to come up with ideas for a scene, and push for the script to be changed by using language such as "We need to," and "We have to try this..." A fast decision maker, Carrey often jumps to quick conclusions both on and off the set. The lifelong comedian is an excellent storyteller and generally talks more than he listens. He is unafraid to get physically close to others with his forward-

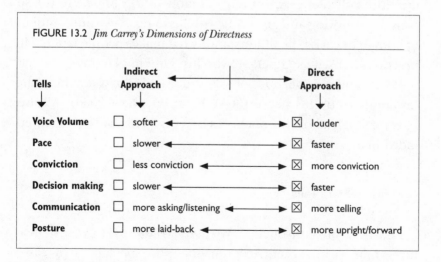

FIGURE 13.2 *Jim Carrey's Dimensions of Directness*

Tells	Indirect Approach		Direct Approach
Voice Volume	☐ softer ◄	─────►	☒ louder
Pace	☐ slower ◄	─────►	☒ faster
Conviction	☐ less conviction ◄	─────►	☒ more conviction
Decision making	☐ slower ◄	─────►	☒ faster
Communication	☐ more asking/listening ◄	─────►	☒ more telling
Posture	☐ more laid-back ◄	─────►	☒ more upright/forward

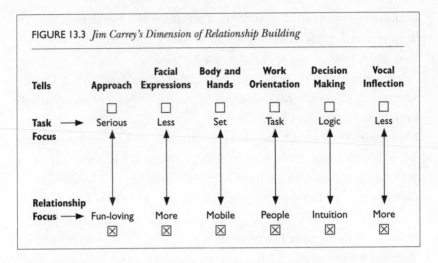

FIGURE 13.3 *Jim Carrey's Dimension of Relationship Building*

Tells	Approach	Facial Expressions	Body and Hands	Work Orientation	Decision Making	Vocal Inflection
	☐	☐	☐	☐	☐	☐
Task Focus ⟶	Serious	Less	Set	Task	Logic	Less
Relationship Focus ⟶	Fun-loving	More	Mobile	People	Intuition	More
	☒	☒	☒	☒	☒	☒

leaning posture has led to many humorous scenes. In all six behavior clusters, Carrey falls on the direct side of this dimension.

Looking at the dimension of relationship building, Figure 13.3, it's easy to see that Carrey is a fun-loving individual. He gains satisfaction from making others laugh. He has been labeled "aggressively infantile," and "gleefully uninhibited." As he was growing up, Carrey's mother was often ill, and sometimes bedridden. From an early age, he did impersonations and told jokes to make her laugh and brighten her day. He often contorts his malleable face into ridiculous expressions, notably in *The Mask*. He is also constantly moving and gesturing with his hands. An astute student of human behavior, he understands what makes people laugh. He describes himself as "a person who just kind of like throws myself out there and does all kinds of wild stuff," and admits that he wears his emotions on his sleeve (Steve Kroft interview, 2006). All this information leads us to conclude Carrey is a relationship-oriented individual.

Additional Style Tells

Carrey's breakthrough movie, *Ace Ventura: Pet Detective*, features him as an eccentric gumshoe who specializes in cases involving animals. Ace is easily identified by his bright Hawaiian shirts and an eye-catching hairdo. Bright clothing and interesting hair styles can often be a tell for an Extrovert.

A huge fan of professional wrestling, Carrey relates to the showmanship of the sport, even once shaving his head to look like his favorite wrestler. Extroverts often can relate to other performers and are willing to take risks, including making fashion statements.

Extroverts tend to be creative: Carrey has said, "I like being creative, basically, period." (Steve Kroft interview, 2004)

Results of Jim Carrey's Style Analysis

Looking at the styles scorecard in Figure 13.4, we can see Jim Carrey falls on the direct side of the first dimension and the relationship-oriented side of the second dimension. Using this information, we can determine Carrey's dominant style.

Carrey is a classic Extrovert. Gregarious, outgoing and in love with the spotlight, he talks loudly, laughs often and exudes enthusiasm and energy.

In the next section, you will practice determining the dominant style of four individuals.

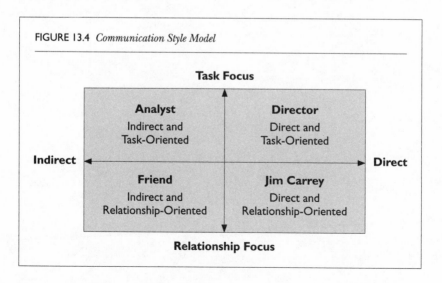

FIGURE 13.4 *Communication Style Model*

Task Focus

Analyst	Director
Indirect and Task-Oriented	Direct and Task-Oriented

Indirect ← → **Direct**

Friend	Jim Carrey
Indirect and Relationship-Oriented	Direct and Relationship-Oriented

Relationship Focus

STYLES READING SKILL PRACTICE

Apply the method described above to the four well-known personalities below. If you're not familiar with a name, proceed to the next example. Remember, this is practice: Just as with any new skill, it is difficult to do it perfectly the first time. Simply do your best. Go behavior by behavior for each of the two dimensions for each individual starting with Mike Wallace, the former CBS newscaster. Check each behavior you think that person exhibits. Start with vocal volume: does the person have a softer voice or a louder one? Check the corresponding box, and then move through the rest of the behaviors.

Once you complete the styles scorecard, write down any additional styles tells, or other characteristic behaviors this individual exhibits. Lastly, based on our answers and observations make an educated guess as to the style of the individual.

After (and only after!) you write down your guess of the style, check the next page to find (an analysis of the dominant style of the individual) the accurately, completed styles scorecard, and additional styles tell.

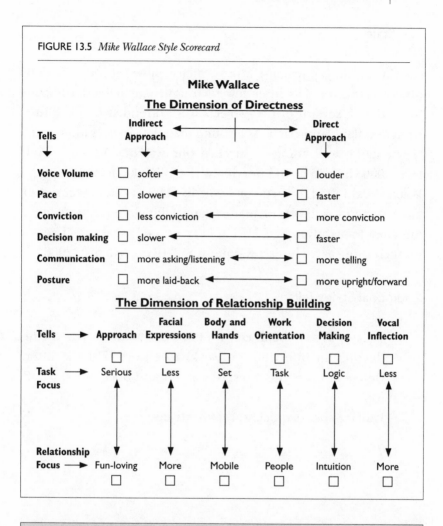

FIGURE 13.5 *Mike Wallace Style Scorecard*

Additional Styles Tells:

_____

_____

_____

The Style:

_____

The Style

Hard-hitting journalist Mike Wallace, now retired, was definitely a Director. His interview technique was legendarily confrontational; several of his subjects were offended by his blunt, straight-talking approach. As a young man, he was very ambitious: "I was damn well going to succeed one way or another," (Wallace, 2006) he said in an interview with CBS. Like many Directors, Wallace exhibited a need for control: He was often accused of ambushing his subjects or manipulating the circumstances of an interview to his advantage. He has been quoted as saying, "There's no such thing as an indiscreet question." (Ryan, August, 2006)

Additional Styles Tells

- Wallace likes to be in control of most situations: When conducting an interview, he works to ensure that the interviewee answers the questions asked and does not stray off topic.
- Wallace speaks quickly and assertively.

FIGURE 13.6 *Style Scorecard for Mike Wallace*

Mike Wallace

The Dimension of Directness

Tells	Indirect Approach		Direct Approach

Voice Volume	☐ softer	◄————► ☒	louder
Pace	☐ slower	◄————► ☒	faster
Conviction	☐ less conviction	◄————► ☒	more conviction
Decision making	☐ slower	◄————► ☒	faster
Communication	☐ more asking/listening	◄————► ☒	more telling
Posture	☐ more laid-back	◄————► ☒	more upright/forward

The Dimension of Relationship Building

Tells ➤	Approach	Facial Expressions	Body and Hands	Work Orientation	Decision Making	Vocal Inflection
	☒	☒	☒	☒	☒	☒
Task Focus ➤	Serious	Less	Set	Task	Logic	Less
	▲	▲	▲	▲	▲	▲
	▼	▼	▼	▼	▼	▼
Relationship Focus ➤	Fun-loving	More	Mobile	People	Intuition	More
	☐	☐	☐	☐	☐	☐

FIGURE 13.7 *Anthony Robbins Style Scorecard*

Anthony Robbins
The Dimension of Directness

Tells

Indirect Approach ⟷ | ⟷ Direct Approach

	Indirect Approach		Direct Approach
Voice Volume	☐ softer	⟷	☐ louder
Pace	☐ slower	⟷	☐ faster
Conviction	☐ less conviction	⟷	☐ more conviction
Decision making	☐ slower	⟷	☐ faster
Communication	☐ more asking/listening	⟷	☐ more telling
Posture	☐ more laid-back	⟷	☐ more upright/forward

The Dimension of Relationship Building

Tells ➤	Approach	Facial Expressions	Body and Hands	Work Orientation	Decision Making	Vocal Inflection
	☐	☐	☐	☐	☐	☐
Task Focus ➤	Serious	Less	Set	Task	Logic	Less
	↕	↕	↕	↕	↕	↕
Relationship Focus ➤	Fun-loving	More	Mobile	People	Intuition	More
	☐	☐	☐	☐	☐	☐

Additional Styles Tells:

_____

_____

The Style:

_____

The Style

Anthony Robbins is a best-selling self-help author, motivational speaker, and advisor to world leaders, sports professionals, and businesspeople. An internationally recognized personality, he has appeared on countless infomercials, television interviews, talk shows, and radio programs. In his motivational seminars he often thrusts his fist into the air, soaks participants with water guns, and moves around the stage with boundless energy. Robbins's fast-paced nature, high-energy character, and focus on the power of the mind to overcome life's obstacles make him an enthusiastic Extrovert.

Additional Styles Tells

- Robbins talks fast and use lots of vocal inflection.
- He uses a variety of facial expressions and hand gestures; you can almost always tell how he is feeling.
- Robbins likes being the center of attention, and shares personal stories to connect with and motivate others.

FIGURE 13.8 *Style Scorecard for Anthony Robbins*

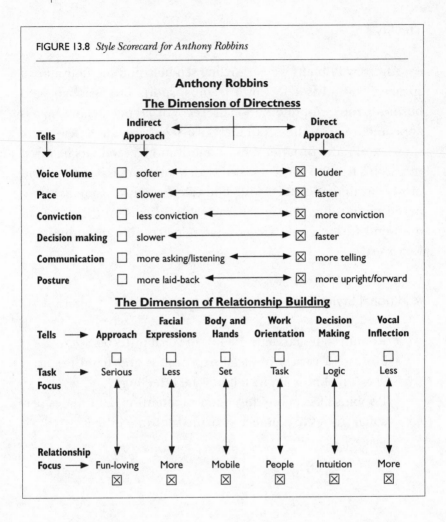

Anthony Robbins

The Dimension of Directness

Tells	Indirect Approach		Direct Approach

Voice Volume	☐ softer	←————————→	☒ louder
Pace	☐ slower	←————————→	☒ faster
Conviction	☐ less conviction	←————————→	☒ more conviction
Decision making	☐ slower	←————————→	☒ faster
Communication	☐ more asking/listening	←————————→	☒ more telling
Posture	☐ more laid-back	←————————→	☒ more upright/forward

The Dimension of Relationship Building

Tells →	Approach	Facial Expressions	Body and Hands	Work Orientation	Decision Making	Vocal Inflection
	☐	☐	☐	☐	☐	☐
Task Focus →	Serious	Less	Set	Task	Logic	Less
	↕	↕	↕	↕	↕	↕
Relationship Focus →	Fun-loving	More	Mobile	People	Intuition	More
	☒	☒	☒	☒	☒	☒

FIGURE 13.9 *Mr. Spock Style Scorecard*

Mr. Spock of *Star Trek*
The Dimension of Directness

Tells	Indirect Approach		Direct Approach

Voice Volume	☐ softer	⟷	☐ louder
Pace	☐ slower	⟷	☐ faster
Conviction	☐ less conviction	⟷	☐ more conviction
Decision making	☐ slower	⟷	☐ faster
Communication	☐ more asking/listening	⟷	☐ more telling
Posture	☐ more laid-back	⟷	☐ more upright/forward

The Dimension of Relationship Building

Tells →	Approach	Facial Expressions	Body and Hands	Work Orientation	Decision Making	Vocal Inflection
	☐	☐	☐	☐	☐	☐
Task Focus	Serious	Less	Set	Task	Logic	Less
	↕	↕	↕	↕	↕	↕
Relationship Focus →	Fun-loving	More	Mobile	People	Intuition	More
	☐	☐	☐	☐	☐	☐

Additional Styles Tells:

_____

_____

_____

The Style:

_____

The Style

Spock is half Vulcan and half human and displays the Vulcan tendency to value reason and logic over emotion. His intelligence is based on rational thought, and he generally makes decisions only after considering several factors. Famous for continually having a blank, poker-faced expression, Spock rarely if ever smiles. He is a walking encyclopedia. He weighs the pros and the cons of every option, which can be a challenge if Captain Kirk has to make a quick decision to save the starship. Spock's monotone voice is rarely prone to highs or lows in terms of pitch and pace, which is characteristic of an Analyst. He has emotions, but as a Vulcan, he is wary of them disrupting a logical decision-making process.

Additional Style Tells

- Spock shows very little emotion and has very limited facial expressions.
- Spock speaks slowly and with precision, choosing his words carefully.

FIGURE 13.10 *Style Scorecard for Mr. Spock*

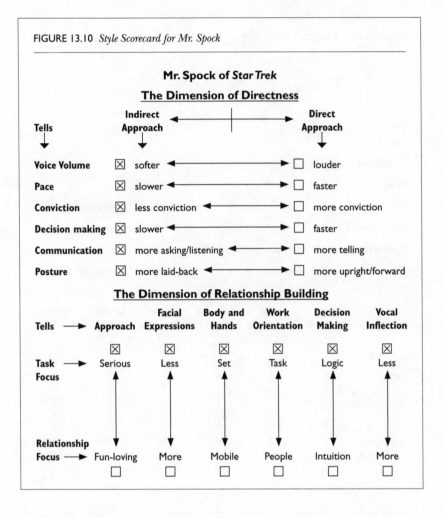

FIGURE 13.11 *Katie Couric Style Scorecard*

Katie Couric

The Dimension of Directness

Tells	Indirect Approach		Direct Approach

Voice Volume	☐ softer ◄────────────►	☐ louder
Pace	☐ slower ◄────────────►	☐ faster
Conviction	☐ less conviction ◄────────────►	☐ more conviction
Decision making	☐ slower ◄────────────►	☐ faster
Communication	☐ more asking/listening ◄────────────►	☐ more telling
Posture	☐ more laid-back ◄────────────►	☐ more upright/forward

The Dimension of Relationship Building

Tells ➤	Approach	Facial Expressions	Body and Hands	Work Orientation	Decision Making	Vocal Inflection
	☐	☐	☐	☐	☐	☐
Task Focus	Serious	Less	Set	Task	Logic	Less
	↕	↕	↕	↕	↕	↕
Relationship Focus ➤	Fun-loving	More	Mobile	People	Intuition	More
	☐	☐	☐	☐	☐	☐

Additional Styles Tells:

_____

_____

_____

The Style:

_____

The Style

Katie Couric gained fame as the cohost of NBC's *Today Show.* In 2006 she began anchoring the CBS *Evening News,* making her the first female solo anchor of a major U.S. TV network weekday evening newscast. Early in her career Couric gained fame by building strong bonds with her interviewees. Couric's slow, reassuring voice facilitates comfort, empathy and trust with her interviewees. International political figures and celebrities have asked for Couric to interview them when they are grappling with difficult issues or wish to share personal information with the public. One of only five women that *Time* magazine has repeatedly ranked among the world's most influential people, Couric is an effective listener, rarely interrupting others or pushing interviewees to answer uncomfortable questions. She shares her life with her audience, going so far as to undergo a colonoscopy on-air in March 2000 to increase funding for cancer research and to educate the public on cancer prevention. She has called her crusade against cancer her proudest achievement. Friends are defined by their ability to bond with others and connect with people.

We hope that you had some success in your first attempt at reading styles, and that we answered any questions you had. As with all the skills you will learn from this book, please remember this key self-talk phrase: "Improvement, not perfection."

Additional Style Tells

- Couric is noted for regularly saying "Thank you so much," and for her warm smile.
- Couric often asks interviewees personal questions and is usually forthcoming about her own feelings and concerns.

FIGURE 13.12 *Style Scorecard for Katie Couric*

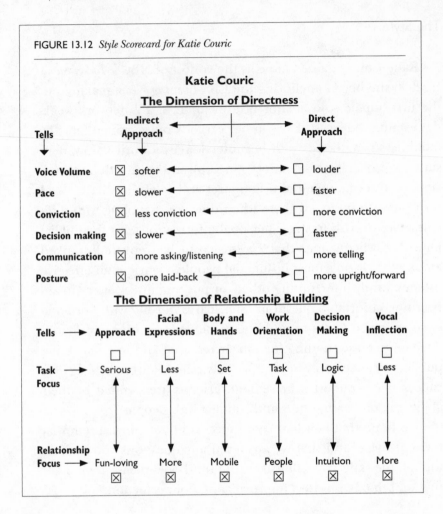

Katie Couric

The Dimension of Directness

	Indirect Approach		Direct Approach
Tells →			
Voice Volume	☒ softer ◄───────►	☐	louder
Pace	☒ slower ◄───────►	☐	faster
Conviction	☒ less conviction ◄───────►	☐	more conviction
Decision making	☒ slower ◄───────►	☐	faster
Communication	☒ more asking/listening ◄───────►	☐	more telling
Posture	☒ more laid-back ◄───────►	☐	more upright/forward

The Dimension of Relationship Building

Tells →	Approach	Facial Expressions	Body and Hands	Work Orientation	Decision Making	Vocal Inflection
Task Focus →	☐ Serious	☐ Less	☐ Set	☐ Task	☐ Logic	☐ Less
Relationship Focus →	Fun-loving ☒	More ☒	Mobile ☒	People ☒	Intuition ☒	More ☒

ADDITIONAL TIPS ON READING STYLES

In our seminars we often hear the question, "How do I know that what I'm observing is really a person's communication habit? Maybe he or she is just in a mood." This is possible, but fairly unlikely. Remember, 80 to 90 percent of our behavior is habit. Also, it's unlikely that a customer will try to fool you by behaving outside his or her comfort zone: As you probably have noticed, customers rarely go out of their way to change their natural behavior to try and adapt to you! There is a high likelihood that the behavior a customer exhibits is a real communication style tell.

You may encounter people who are truly difficult to read. Even when you use the styles scorecard and the additional styles tells, this person seems so balanced that he or she has no dominant style. In this case, you are either dealing with a person who is extremely balanced naturally, or who is self-trained to be balanced. Don't worry about these folks too much: They are generally very easy to get along with and, at times, actually adapt their behavior to yours rather than vice versa.

During the styles reading practices, you may have thought, "I don't always have enough time to gather this much information on a customer," or, "To read people correctly, there are so many things to think about." First, some interactions are shorter than others; focus on doing the best you can. Second, it requires practice to pick up the styles and categorize them effectively. Once you get the hang of it, though, the payoff is very high. The good news is that, as with all other habits, once you acquire them, they stay with you and become both easy and efficient. Professionals we have trained who committed to learning and practicing these styles say that styles tells have begun to jump out at them as if they were in neon. With your commitment, the same will happen for you.

Finally, don't limit your practice only to customers, especially at first. As with all the skills in this book, you can practice reading styles tells every time you interact with someone. Try it with your coworkers, friends, and family. You can even try applying it to TV characters; you will find many of them have a distinct style as well.

14

ADAPTING
TO STYLES

Now that you understand the four styles and how to read them, we will discuss each style in depth and provide the crucial tools you need to adapt your behavior to your customer's. In this chapter we discuss the following subjects:

- *The key don'ts, or behaviors to avoid.* How to avoid behaviors that are most likely to frustrate people of a particular style.
- *Missing the tells and an example of not adapting.* A scenario showing what might occur if we miss tells and don't adapt to them.
- *The key dos, or behaviors to engage in.* Behaviors that put people of each style in their comfort zones, cultivating trust and openness.
- *Reading the tells and an example of successful adaptation.* A scenario showing what can happen when we read the tells and adapt.
- *Red flags.* People from each style have a unique way of expressing frustration and mistrust. We show you each style's most common red flags or signals of frustration.

- *Self-talk to help you adapt to styles.* Key self-talk phrases to motivate you to adapt to each style and to keep you in a positive frame of mind while adapting.

ADAPTING TO ANALYSTS

Key Don'ts with Analysts

- *Fast pace.* You will frustrate Analysts by speaking fast and not giving them sufficient time to ask questions or process information. Remember, Analysts value precision and accuracy. They like to explore all their options in order to reduce risk and make the best possible decision. If you speak quickly or don't listen well, (through interrupting or neglecting to restate their concerns), they will perceive you as pushy or inconsiderate.
- *Passion and enthusiasm.* You might think, "How could passion and enthusiasm ever be negative qualities when interacting with a customer?" With the Analyst, however, too much enthusiasm may actually create mistrust. Analysts often believe emotion, feelings, and subjectivity are weaknesses that prevent sound decision making. Therefore, it's not a good idea to use animated face and hand gestures, or language such as, "this will be the best decision you ever made," "this will work wonders," "this is the best product I have ever seen," or "I really feel this is right for you." If analysts hear these phrases they may think that you have an agenda and are trying to sell them something and you will lose their trust. If an Analyst refers to you as a *salesperson*, this is not a compliment. Although people of all styles are constantly judging whether you have their best interest in mind or you're trying to push your own agenda, Analysts are particularly sensitive to it.

- *Personal connection.* As we previously mentioned, Analysts are usually not interested in forging a bond immediately. They may find personal questions or personal information about you to be intrusive, rude, and inappropriate unless they have solicited it. Analysts like their personal space—most are not comfortable with touch or close physical proximity when you are interacting with them.

Scenario: A Car Sale Gone Wrong

This scenario is an example of a customer service interaction in which a well-intentioned customer service professional frustrates an Analyst customer by committing Analyst-specific don'ts.

The Analytical guest, David, has just gotten out of his car at a local car dealership. In his hands are some papers. He is immediately approached by Victoria, an Extrovert salesperson who is very happy to see him. Her bright tone and loud voice seem to startle him.

Victoria: "Well, hello there! Welcome to the city's best car dealership!"

She reaches out and puts a hand on his shoulder. He backs away. As she continues to speak, he hugs his paperwork close to his body and begins to pace nervously on the spot.

Victoria: "Are you ready to find the vehicle of your dreams today?"

David looks down at his papers for reference and opens his mouth to say something, but Victoria just keeps on talking. David closes his mouth and starts shaking his head a little. He even covers his mouth with his hand, as if he is holding himself back from speaking.

Victoria, gesturing with her hands: "We have endless sedans, minivans, SUVs, sports cars, even convertibles. Which one is calling you?"

David, looking at his papers and looking her in the eyes: "Well, actually, I'm here to explore my options about this flier that I received."

David, making small, contained gestures: "According to this, you offer some 2005 models…"

Victoria leans in to look at the papers, putting her hand on his arm. He hesitates and takes a step back. She steps in again and rests her fingertips on his arm. He moves away again.

David: "…that, if bought by Sunday, will include an extended warranty of an additional 30,000 miles at no additional charge. Is that an additional 30,000 miles on a specific number of miles, or is it based on the amount of miles the car has on it currently? Can you explain this to me in more detail? And how many of these vehicles do you have in stock?"

Victoria: "I don't have the exact breakdown, but I'm pretty sure it means most of them. In fact, I think there is some variety of a deal on virtually all our vehicles."

She gives him a playful nudge. He begins to shake his head and keeps trying to speak, but she won't give him an opening. Her gestures are expansive, and she stands very close to him.

Victoria: "I'd say, let's just get started with what you like, what jumps out at you. Trust your gut! I'm sure it will be the right deal in the end."

At this, David grimaces and shakes his head.

David, referring to his paperwork again: "Well, but this ad says only certain vehicles for certain times, and I want to make sure I have all the facts straight and take full advantage of this ad."

She leans into him again and puts a friendly arm around his shoulder.

David, shrugging with frustration and backing up: "I just need to have all this explained to me."

Victoria: "Sir, as I said before, we have fantastic deals on just about all the vehicles! Don't get stuck in the details, focus on which vehicle feels right for you, and you'll get a good deal—trust me! Now, where would you like to start? Actually, I think I have just the car for you."

She starts to walk toward the lot. Now he holds his hand up to stop her.

David: "You know, actually, I'd like to think about it for a while, and I'll be back, OK?"

He turns back and walks toward his car.

David, under his breath: "What a salesperson!"

What went wrong—learning opportunities. This is one version of a classic scenario we have seen many times: an Extrovert trying to effectively communicate with an Analyst without adapting to the Analyst's tells. Victoria did all the right things to please another Extrovert; she was energetic, enthusiastic, tactile, fast-paced, assertive, and positive. She focused on emotion and intuition. These behaviors, unfortunately, have a negative impact when used with an Analyst. Her effusive welcome, exaggerated language, and physical closeness made David uncomfortable. She displayed behavior that would work for her, emphasizing emotion, focusing on the bigger picture, and moving fast. Her behavior not only made the Analyst uncomfortable, but also frustrated him and eroded his trust in her.

To Dos with Analysts

- *Slow your pace.* The first step to successfully interacting with Analysts is to slow your pace so that they do not feel rushed. They must trust that you are careful, thoughtful, and willing to give them time to ask questions and process information.
- *Formal and calm.* To meet Analysts in their comfort zone, tone down your body language, gesticulations, and facial expressions.
- *Precise language.* Avoid using generalized, exaggerated language; use more precise, factual language. Also, ensure that you list both the pros and cons of an idea.
- *Invitational language.* Convey the message, "I have not yet decided what the right answer for you is. I'm here with an open mind to give you all the information you need so that you can make an informed decision." Choosing the right language is critical when interacting with a customer. With

the Analyst, the following invitational phrases allow you to state your thoughts while maintaining an open and collaborative stance.

- One alternative...
- One option I see...
- What are your thoughts on this possibility?
- What if...
- *Documentation.* Whenever possible, gather documentation. Analysts desire data and facts.
- *Reduce risk.* Try to demonstrate to Analysts that the decisions they are making are low risk.

Scenario: A Car Sale Done Right

In this scenario we detail a similar interaction to the one above, but this time our Extrovert picks up on the signals and adapts her behavior to the Analyst's.

Victoria: "Welcome to our dealership, how may I be of service?"

David looks down at his papers for reference, pauses for a moment to think and then says: "Well, actually, I'm here to explore my options about this flier that I received. According to this, there are some 2005 models that, if bought by Sunday, include an extended warranty of an additional 30,000 miles at no additional cost. Is that an additional 30,000 miles on a specific number of miles, or is it based on the amount of miles the car currently has? Can you explain this to me in more detail? And how many of these vehicles do you have in stock?"

Victoria waits patiently for David to finish speaking before she begins to talk.

Victoria, in a calm and deliberate tone: "It's my understanding that the 30,000 miles is in addition to the original factory warranty of 30,000 miles, meaning that each of the vehicles in this category now have a warranty of 60,000 miles. Does this answer your first question?"

David: "Yes, it does."

Victoria: "In response to your second question about the number of these vehicles we have in stock, I'm not sure of the exact number we currently have, because we are continuously selling them. If you like, I would be glad to get you the latest report on what we have in stock."

David: "That would be good."

Victoria: "While I'm generating the reports, is there any additional information I can provide that might help you in your search, such as the make, color, price, or mileage of the vehicles?"

David: "That would be excellent. I am particularly interested in mileage and price."

Victoria: "No problem. I'll be back with that data shortly."

Victoria returns and hands David the report that lists the vehicles and their price and mileage.

Victoria: "Does this have all the information you were looking for?"

David: "Yes, this is very useful; this is the key information for my decision-making process. Where do you think I should start?"

Victoria: "One possibility would be to look at them in order of lowest to highest mileage, and then you could compare mileage to price."

David: "Good, let's do that."

What went right?—analyzing success. In this second scenario, Victoria has redeemed herself. She did an excellent job of picking up on the Analyst's tells and adapting her approach. Specifically, she slowed down her pace, remained calm, gave the Analyst time to process and think, provided details, and checked to make sure the Analyst had all the information he needed to proceed. Eventually, the Analyst actually asked Victoria for advice on where to start. Many times Analysts become open to your suggestions and advice once they trust you. That is why it's crucial to adapt early in your interaction with an Analyst; it dramatically increases your odds of building trust. Although you may have to be extra patient at the beginning of the interaction, it pays off in the end.

Red Flags for Analysts

- *Nit-picking.* Analysts fall on the indirect side of the Communication Styles Model, and therefore are not comfortable with conflict, preferring to assert themselves through questions. If they feel they are being rushed or "sold," they ask questions about minutiae to slow you down.
- *Shutting down.* By nature Analysts are not confrontational. If they become aggravated or angry, they simply stop talking. If an Analyst stops paying attention, contributing to the conversation, and asking questions, this may well be the reason why.
- *Sarcasm.* Analysts also show their frustration through sarcasm. Often their sarcastic comments can tell you exactly how the Analyst is feeling.

If you catch any of these signs, slow down and find out what the problem is. You could use phrases such as the following:

- I've given you a lot of information. Let me stop and ask if you have any questions or concerns.
- Have I missed anything of importance to you?
- Are there any risks that haven't been addressed?

ADAPTING TO DIRECTORS

Key Don'ts with Directors

- *Small talk.* Perhaps the fastest way to frustrate Directors is by not addressing their requests once they have made them clear. Try not to make small talk. While some styles appreciate your willingness to connect personally, it may frustrate Directors.
- *Talking slowly and too much.* Directors are almost always in a hurry. If you speak slowly or in great detail, telling anecdotes

or personal stories before you have addressed their needs, you likely will frustrate them. Their self-talk at that moment might sound like this: "You're confusing me with somebody who cares!" or "Please, get to the point already!"

- *Telling them what to do.* Of all the communication styles, Directors have the highest need for control, and become irritated if they feel they're being told what to do. If you use language such as "You should," "Obviously," "Logically," or "This is a no-brainer," they will resist and perhaps get angry.

Scenario: Jim Gets Too Friendly

Below is a scenario in which a Director, Tom, walks into a clothing store and is greeted by a customer service professional, Jim, a Friend. Jim does not adapt to Tom's style.

Jim: "Good evening, sir."

Tom: "Good evening."

Jim: "Did you have any trouble finding us?"

Tom: "No."

Jim: "Are you from the area or are you from out of town? We get plenty of business travelers coming through."

Tom, frowning slightly: "I'm here on business."

Jim: "Interesting. So where is home for you?"

Tom, abruptly: "Orlando, Florida."

Jim: "No kidding! I just took my wife and kids down to Disney World. What a great time we had. The kids are already begging me for the next trip. Have you ever been to Disney World?"

Tom, impatiently: "Yes. So, I'm looking for a black, cotton sports coat."

Jim, speaking slowly: "Sure. There is nothing like a black sports coat. That sounds like an excellent choice. But I just want to make you aware that we also have a great selection of gray and navy sports coats, and we have a special on woven ties. I'd be glad to take you to see them. In fact, I just bought several of the ties myself last week and I've gotten a number of compliments—"

Tom, interrupting him in frustration: "Actually, I just need a black sports coat."

Jim: "OK, no problem. Follow me."

Tom, with urgency: "This way?"

Jim: "Yes."

They walk together.

Jim: "So, what business are you in, sir? Do you travel often?"

Tom: "Real estate, and yeah."

Jim: "Ah, real estate. Now, there is a great business."

Tom raises his eyebrows and looks at the floor as if to say, "Here he goes again."

Jim: "You know, I was in real estate for a while, and I really enjoyed working with people, the interaction—"

Tom, interrupting and exasperated: "Are these the sport coats here?"

Jim: "Yes, this is our selection."

Tom begins looking through the rack.

Jim: "Is there anything else I can do for you? Can I get you anything?"

Tom: "I'm fine. I'm all set."

Jim: "OK. Have a great day."

Jim leaves and Tom shakes his head.

Tom, muttering: "Yeah. I might be able to now."

What went wrong?—learning opportunities. It's clear that this was not a successful conversation. The question is: what went wrong? Jim was friendly and positive. He tried to build a rapport with Tom. He gave Tom a variety of options. Aren't all these useful techniques when conversing with a customer? It depends on the customer. With a Director they're not only useless, but worse, they can potentially backfire. If you refer back to the list of don'ts for the Director, you can see that all the techniques Jim used are triggers for the Director and can result in a frustrating experience.

To Dos with Directors

- *Get down to business.* Directors usually have a specific purpose in mind. Because of their fast-paced nature, it is crucial to find out that purpose fast, and then show that you are pursuing it quickly. Directors greatly appreciate your focus and efficiency.

- *Less is more.* Be as concise in your speech as possible. Directors are very clear about their needs, so you don't necessarily need to give them all the possible options and details. Respond to what they are asking; if they need more information they won't be shy about asking for it. You risk frustrating them if you say too much. Remember to answer their questions rather than simply focusing on what you want to talk about.

- *Language of conviction.* Directors usually think of themselves as confident, and they respond best to other confident people. If you use language that is weak, such as: "Would it be silly if," or "This isn't really my area of expertise, but…" they may dismiss you as having no credibility. On the other hand, if you use pushy-sounding or dictatorial words, they will want to take control. Directors want the best of your thinking, but not shoved down their throats. They want you to be confident but not cocky when making suggestions. Below are the phrases we recommend to achieve this impression when engaging a Director:
  - My point of view…
  - Based on my experience…
  - This is your decision, but if it was mine I would…
  - I recommend…
  - I suggest…
  - My advice would be…

Scenario: Jim Gets to the Point

Here is another version of the interaction between Tom and Jim; this time Jim adapts his behavior appropriately.

Jim: "Good evening sir, how may I help you?"

Tom: "I am looking for a black sport coat."

Jim: "OK, I'll take you to that section of the store. Right this way."

They begin walking over to the sports section of the store.

Jim, turning his attention toward Tom: "Did you have a particular fabric in mind? We have a couple of options."

Tom: "I usually go with wool, but what else do you have?"

Jim: "We do carry them in wool, but we also have some in cotton, polyester, and linen."

Tom: "I will be wearing it a couple of times at a conference this week. You are an expert in clothing, what do you think?"

Jim: "Sir, because it will be a warm week, I would recommend the linen. It is the lightest of the fabrics, it will keep you the coolest, and it's also in style right now."

Tom: "I do tend to get hot at these events; that sounds like a good solution. Let's look at what you have in a 34 regular."

What went right—analyzing success. As you can see, Jim's second approach led to a far more positive customer service interaction. He used crisp language and got to the point quickly, appealing to the Director's need for efficiency and timeliness. Another skillful tactic of Jim's was discovering Tom's priority without first spending time trying to build rapport. Then he immediately started walking Tom toward the sport coat section. This action met two of the Director's key needs: it allowed Tom to state his priority, and let Jim demonstrate that he was focused on it. Once Jim had moved Tom into his comfort zone, he listed Tom's options in terms of sport coats. Now Tom was open to hearing them, and appreciated the information.

It's crucial to distinguish between the way Jim offered the Director options in the first scenario, which caused friction, and in the second scenario, which made the interaction successful. In the first scenario, Jim began giving Tom options before he had clearly demonstrated that he was focused on Tom's priority, making Tom lose patience and become frustrated. In the second scenario, Jim showed he was focused on Tom's priority, a black sports coat, and that he was actively moving toward it. Directors do want options sometimes; as a customer service professional, you might be compelled to provide them immediately, but it's most important to determine their priority and show you are focused on it. You can then provide options. When Tom asked Jim for his opinion on which sports coat to choose, Jim did not use strong language that could trigger the Director's need for control (such as "Obviously..." or "The clear choice..."), but by using the phrase "I recommend..." he demonstrated confidence and met Tom in his comfort zone.

Red Flags for Directors

- *Appearing distracted.* Generally, because Directors don't mind confrontation and conflict, it's not difficult to see when they are upset—they will tell you! There are, however, early warning signs of impending anger, such as impatience. They might seem distracted or look at their watches while you are speaking.
- *Interrupting.* If you find a Director finishing your sentences or cutting you off, immediately refocus on the Director's priority and demonstrate your desire to execute it quickly.

ADAPTING TO FRIENDS

Key Don'ts for Friends

- *Resist connection.* More than any other style, Friends value personal connection. If they feel you are rushing them, not interested in small talk, brushing aside their questions, or ignoring their attempts to create a bond, you will quickly create ill will and mistrust.

- *Sarcasm.* Friends are often very sensitive to the feelings of others; sarcasm, locker-room banter, or poking fun at people may make Friends think you are insensitive.
- *Rushing business.* Friends may react adversely if they sense you are trying to rush or push them toward business. They may feel like you don't care and that they're just a number to you.

Scenario: A Big Menu Causes a Big Problem

In the following scenario, Brigitte, a Friend, seeks help from Don, a waiter and Director who doesn't understand the above don'ts. Brigitte enters the restaurant, sits at a table, and looks at the menu. After a few minutes Don comes over to the table.

Don: "Good evening, ma'am, have you decided what you would like?"

Brigitte: "Actually, no. It's my first time at your restaurant. Your menu is very large and a little bit overwhelming. If my son Jeff were here he would probably know what to order, he's got a real knack for that, but he and his friends decided to skip dinner. Do you have any kids?"

Don: "Yes, I have one."

Don pauses briefly.

Don: "Do you know what you would like to order?"

Brigitte holds her palms up helplessly. Her facial expression as she speaks is animated, and her tone of voice is lively.

Brigitte: "I'm having a hard time deciding. Are there certain house specialties I just have to try? What are the portion sizes like? What do you suggest?"

Don, in a straightforward, unemotional voice: "The rib eye is the special. And the portion sizes are all fairly large. Do you have any other questions?"

Brigitte: "No, I suppose not, I mean—I'm on vacation. And this is precious time. So I want to make sure that during these dinners out I'm ordering the right dishes."

Don: "OK."

Again, Don pauses for a moment.

Don: "So, are you ready to order or should I come back in a few minutes?"

Brigitte: "Actually, I think I do need some time."

Don walks away from the table.

Brigitte, rolling her eyes and adopting a sarcastic tone: "Not too friendly around here, I guess."

What went wrong—learning opportunities. You might be thinking, "What did this waiter do wrong? He was attentive, he gave Brigitte what she wanted, and he didn't interrupt—what is the problem?" We agree that he didn't provide terrible customer service. Excellent service, however, requires reading tells and adapting to the specific needs of the customer. This is what Don failed to do. Because he failed to pick up Brigitte's tells, he didn't meet this Friend in her comfort zone. Brigitte tried to bond with Don by asking him about his kids and his own favorite dishes. Don stayed focused on the task at hand—taking Brigitte's order. As a result, Brigitte felt Don was impersonal and uncaring.

To Dos with Friends

- *Take the time to bond.* We're not suggesting that you tell your life story or reveal intimate secrets: Simply take the time to answer questions in depth, and perhaps ask a few questions in return. This can be done in a matter of minutes.
- *Smile.* Friends are warm, open people and they appreciate people similar to them. A smile is one of the quickest and most efficient ways to show you are interested in them.
- *Slow your pace.* To meet Friends in their comfort zone, slow your speech.

- *Focus on people.* Whenever you explain a concept to Friends, focus on how it will impact people and relationships. If they see that you are considerate of them and are factoring them into your thought process, you build trust and make a positive impression.
- *Invitational language.* Like Analysts, Friends respond most effectively to invitational rather than demanding or directive language. Just as they are uncomfortable pressuring others to make choices, they themselves do not like to feel forced into a decision. Invitational phrases provide information without making Friends feel pressured. They include:
  - One alternative...
  - One option I see...
  - What are your thoughts on this possibility?
  - What if...
- *Pick up on their hints.* Many Friends present their ideas indirectly, saying, "I wonder how it would work if..." or "Have they ever offered..." This is their way of communicating something important to them, or something they want you to do. Take the hint.

Scenario: A Big Menu Is a Big Opportunity

In the next scenario, Don picks up on the Friend's tells and skillfully adapts his behavior.

Don: "Good evening, ma'am, my name is Don. I will be your server tonight. How has your day been so far?"

Brigitte: "Good evening to you, Don, my name is Brigitte—nice to meet you. It has been a wonderful day, actually. I have taken some vigorous nature hikes and enjoy the beautiful outdoors around here."

Don: "Great, I'm glad to hear your day has been so satisfying. Did you work up a healthy appetite?"

Brigitte: "I definitely did, and so I am hoping you can help me with this menu. It's my first time at your restaurant and your menu is very large and a little bit overwhelming. If my son Jeff were here he would probably know what to order, he's got a real knack for that, but he and his friends decided to skip dinner. Do you have any kids?

Don: "Yes, I have a little girl. She just turned four last week, in fact. It's amazing how fast they grow!"

Brigitte: "It sure is! My kids are 14 and 17 and the years have gone by in a blur!"

They both laugh.

Don: "So, to answer your question, I realize that our menu is very large; perhaps I can point out the house special, and then I'll tell you my personal favorite."

Brigitte: "That would be great!"

Don: "Well, the house specialty is the rib eye, which comes with a choice of steamed veggies, soup, or salad to start. It's quite a bit of food. My personal favorite is the meatloaf; I can't get enough of it."

Brigitte: "Thanks, that helps me. The thing is, I'm on vacation and this is precious time. So I want to make sure that during these dinners out, I'm ordering the right dishes."

Don: "You're on vacation? Where are you from?"

Brigitte: "I live in Minneapolis, so I'm thrilled to be out of the cold!"

Don: "I understand. I moved down here from the Northeast several years ago because I had enough of the cold myself! So, are you ready to order? There is no rush—feel free to take your time."

Brigitte: "Thanks, maybe just a couple more minutes."

Don: "I'll be back."

Don walks away from the table

Brigitte, smiling and content: "Wow, there are some really friendly people around here."

What went right—analyzing success. This is a great example of how picking up tells and being willing to adapt to them can make all the difference. As in the previous scenario, Don's role is to take Brigitte's order. This time, however, he factored in the Friend's need for connection and acted accordingly by introducing himself, asking questions about Brigitte's day and vacation, and sharing a little information about his family. In a matter of minutes, Don satisfied Brigitte's needs.

You may be thinking, "I don't want to get personal with a stranger," or, "My job is very hectic; I don't have time to hang around and chat all day." These are reasonable thoughts. We're not suggesting that you spend huge amounts of time in conversation, and, if you are uncomfortable sharing personal information, you can still ask your customers questions about their lives, their family, their weekend and so forth. In terms of time, you can usually achieve a personal connection with Friends in just a few moments. Remember, Friends are generally very considerate people, especially if they feel you are making an effort. If you encounter a Friend who would like to talk longer than you have time to chat, you can use phrases such as the following:

- It has been great talking with you; unfortunately, I have to attend to the next customer now.
- I am really enjoying our conversation; I need to attend to other customers for now, but I will be glad to come back later when I have more time.

Red Flags for Friends

- *Shutting down.* Yes, even warm, polite Friends get upset. However, because they fall into the more indirect dimension, you might be unable to tell. Perhaps the surest sign that they are frustrated is that they no longer engage in conversation. Try to re-engage them, asking if they have any concerns or if there is any additional information you can provide.
- *Repeating themselves.* Friends repeat questions or comments as a way of saying, "You haven't addressed this issue to my satisfaction," or "You are missing an important point, and our disagreement here may be a deal-breaker." Because Friends

are rarely loud or forceful, you have to pay extra attention to these cues.

- *Mixed signals.* Because Friends are uncomfortable with direct confrontation, they may say something negative, but smile at the same time to soften the message. Conversely, they may say something positive such as "I'm fine with this," but their body language or tone of voice may show no real energy or enthusiasm.

ADAPTING TO EXTROVERTS

Key Don'ts for Extroverts

- *Low energy.* Extroverts thrive on energy, passion, and enthusiasm. If you are emotionally controlled, or even simply laid back, you may turn them off.
- *Not engaging/responding.* Extroverts' habits are often designed to engage others. They expect a response, whether it comes in the form of an interested facial expression, appreciation of their jokes, or a response to their stories. If they don't receive it, they may become frustrated and disillusioned.
- *Negativity.* Extroverts pride themselves on being positive and enthusiastic; negativity turns them off. Avoid being too quick to point out the negative aspects of their ideas.
- *Trying to be the center of attention.* If you try to be funnier or dominate the conversation, you will turn your interaction into a competition.

Scenario: Don't Bet on a Big Tip

In this scenario, Alex, a blackjack dealer and Analyst, fails to adapt his style to his Extrovert customer, Ellen.

Two men sit at a blackjack table. The dealer, Alex, wraps up a hand. Another guest, Ellen, joins the table.

Alex, gathering the cards: "Thank you, gentlemen."

Ellen: "Man, I just came from the Caribbean stud table, and I was hot. I won nearly 500 dollars!"

Alex, without making eye contact: "Please place your bet, ma'am."

Ellen: "I'd like to start off with a bang. Here's my bet."

She pushes her chips playfully across the table.

Ellen: "Deal something good. Blackjack would be fine."

Alex, sarcastically: "Ah, good luck, ma'am."

He deals. Ellen watches him and smiles. The first guest hits, then it is Ellen's turn.

Alex: "Hit or hold, ma'am?"

Ellen: "It depends. What are you going to give me? I'm feeling lucky. This is my lucky shirt. It's all silk, I had it custom-made in New York, and it always brings me luck."

Alex looks away from her and frowns—he's not interested in her story, nor does he believe her shirt is lucky.

Alex: "Well, good luck. Hit or hold, ma'am?"

Ellen, in a dramatic whisper: "I guess I'll hit."

He lays down a card. It's not what she wants. She sags in her chair and lets out a loud sigh.

Ellen: "Well, you can't win them all—although, the same thing happened to me at the Caribbean stud table. I started out slow and then all of a sudden came back with a bang.

She looks expectantly at Alex, waiting for a response. When none comes, she sighs heavily once again. She looks around for reinforcement, but the other players don't meet her eye. Shaking her head and scowling, she leans back in her chair and looks away from the table, letting everyone know that she's now disengaged from the game.

What went wrong—learning opportunities. In this scenario we need to examine what didn't happen, rather than what did. Alex did his job as a dealer. He dealt the cards properly, he asked Ellen if she wanted to hit, he even wished her good luck, and yet, this interaction was less than productive. Alex missed the signals indicating Ellen was looking for engagement and friendliness; he ignored her when she looked to him for a response to her "funny" comments. He also failed to congratulate her when she talked about her winnings, nor did he compliment her custom-made shirt. As a result, Ellen was not a happy Extrovert.

To Dos with Extroverts

- *High energy/fast pace.* Meet Extroverts in their comfort zones by talking faster and raising your energy level.
- *Catch them doing things right.* All communication styles like to receive positive feedback, but Extroverts tend to appreciate it the most. Responding positively to their ideas, their stories, and jokes is one of the best ways to build a positive rapport.
- *Throw ideas around.* These creative, tangential thinkers enjoy brainstorming before making a decision. By giving them time to do so, you bring them into their comfort zone.
- *Breaking new ground.* Extroverts like being original and adventurous. Present cutting-edge ideas; these appeal to them most.

Scenario: Alex Is on a Roll

In the following scenario, Analyst Alex is able to adapt his style to his Extrovert customer's.

Alex, gathering the cards: "Thank you, gentlemen."

Ellen: "Man, I just came from the Caribbean stud table, and I was hot. I won nearly 500 dollars!"

Alex, looking up briefly: "Wow, congratulations! I hope your luck continues here. Please place your bet."

Ellen: "I'd like to start off with a bang. Here's my bet."

She pushes her chips playfully across the table.

Ellen: "Deal something good. Blackjack would be fine."

Alex, with a smile: "I promise to do my best."

He deals. Ellen watches him and smiles. The first guest hits, then it is Ellen's turn.

Alex: "Hit or hold, ma'am?"

Ellen: "It depends. What are you going to give me? I'm feeling lucky. This is my lucky shirt. It's all silk, I had it custom-made in New York, and it always brings me luck."

Alex: "That's a very nice shirt, ma'am; I hope it continues to bring you good luck. Would you like to hit or hold?"

Ellen, in a dramatic whisper: "I guess I'll hit."

He lays down a card. It's not what she wants. She sags in her chair and lets out a loud sigh.

Ellen: "Well, you can't win them all—although, the same thing happened to me at the Caribbean stud table. I started out slow and then all of a sudden came back with a bang."

Alex, with an empathetic smile: "Hard luck ma'am. Maybe this is a good sign, considering what happened at the Caribbean stud table. Just keep focusing on that lucky shirt and it's bound to come through for you."

Ellen, with a smile: "I'm sure you're right! Deal the cards, buddy, I'm getting ready to go on a roll!"

What went right—analyzing success. Alex flexed his style to meet Ellen in her comfort zone without having to change his personality or take much extra time. His adjustments made the difference between a mediocre and exceptional customer service interaction. He picked up her need for engagement and feedback when she first sat down at the table. Meeting this need with eye contact, positive energy, and a brief affirmation, he then proceeded to the task of getting her to place her bet. He continued to give her positive feedback, engage her, and stay positive throughout their interaction while still dealing the cards efficiently. Sometimes people tell us that the trouble with Extroverts is that they talk too much and demand a lot of attention. We hope the example above demonstrates that, in fact, giving Extroverts what they need actually will not take much time, and the payoff is often huge: Extroverts tend to be big spenders and tippers when they are happy.

Red Flags for Extroverts

- *Anger.* Extroverts are usually the most emotional of the four styles. If you use the skills you've learned, you should encourage positive emotions such as enthusiasm and enjoyment. The most common red flag for Extroverts is anger; they might speak loudly, interrupt, curse, or even name-call. Their skin may also flush.
- *Competitiveness.* If Extroverts seem to be competing with you by trying to be funnier, smarter, or more impressive, consider this a red flag, and allow them to win this race. If they feel you are one-upping them, they won't be your customers for long.

ADAPTING YOUR MIND-SET

You need insight and skills in order to flex your style, but it's equally important to cultivate and maintain a positive and open mind. If we aren't prepared and proactive, we may find that people with different styles to our own can trigger us. For example, in a seminar John taught recently, a self-proclaimed Analyst said interacting with an Extrovert made his self-talk negative: "These people are so hard to deal with," he would think. "They are so high maintenance!" This self-talk made him reluctant to interact with the customer at all, much less adapt to him. People of all the different styles have told us many similar stories. Here are some phrases you can use to replace negative self-talk in these situations:

- Everyone has a right to be the style that they are.
- If I take the time to adapt my behavior, my interaction likely will be far more successful and efficient.

- Conflict is oftentimes personality, not personal. I don't take it personally when someone has a different style. It's just the way he or she is.

You don't have to adapt your behavior with everyone you meet; it requires a lot of concentration and effort. Considering, however, that your effectiveness with your customers is such a large part of your success, we highly recommend applying the skills whenever possible.

15

YOUR MOST DIFFICULT STYLE

You are now equipped with all the necessary insights and skills to become an expert in applying the Communication Styles Model. You know the four styles, you are keenly aware of your own style, you can read others' styles, and you know how to adapt. The final chapter in this section examines what predictable advantages and challenges of interacting with the four styles based on your dominant style. This is significant help because when you know the challenges you will likely encounter, you can be that much more prepared for them.

YOU AND THEM

Using the Communication Styles Model is not a perfect science, but it does provide an incredibly valuable guidance system when interacting with customers. Our experience suggests that the style most different from our own is usually the most challenging with which to interact. Not only do we need to move the farthest out of our comfort zone in order to adapt to this style, but we also need to do it while maintaining a positive frame of mind. Now that you know your own style, turn to the part of this chapter that applies to you. That section details how your particular style can further adapt to each of the other styles.

YOU ARE AN ANALYST

Interacting with Another Analyst

Going by the Golden Rule—treat others the way you want to be treated—it's easiest to interact with your own style: You already know what you like. Therefore, behaving in your natural style, while remaining conscious of its dos and don'ts, should work very well.

Interacting with a Friend

You and the Friend are both indirect, so your tone, the pace of your speech, your choice of words, and your skill at listening will match each other well. You do, however, fall on opposite sides of the relationship dimension. Friends like to build personal connections by smiling, being open and talkative, and perhaps asking personal questions. They'll expect the same from you, which may take you out of your task-focused comfort zone. Do your best to adapt to the Friend in these areas.

Interacting with a Director

You are both more task-oriented, so you will both value efficiency, calmness, logic, and reason. However, because you differ on the directness dimension, there are some areas to pay particular attention. First, Directors talk, decide, and generally operate quickly. Quicken your pace, be concise, and act fast. Also, while you may want to provide more options and details, allow them to dictate how much information they want. Finally, to generate trust use language of conviction.

Interacting with an Extrovert

Extroverts differ from you in both dimensions. You are indirect and task-oriented; they are direct and relationship-oriented. This is the style to which you'll probably find it hardest to adapt. Speed up your pace, bring up your energy level, and express enthusiasm by increasing your vocal inflection and showing more facial expressions. Take the time to listen to their stories and jokes, and remember they particularly enjoy positive feedback.

YOU ARE A DIRECTOR

Interacting with Another Director

The Golden Rule applies again here; also remember to listen actively. Directors have a tendency to want to control a conversation; allow this to happen. As a Director you likely have a tendency to use strong, directive language. Be aware of this tendency—it can get you in trouble with another Director if you overdo it. Instead, use language that is confident but not pushy. And allow your customer to have control of the situation.

Interacting with an Extrovert

You have the direct dimension in common, which means your pace, word choice, and body language should match. You'll want to be brief, concise, and quick to get down to business. Extroverts, however, need some informal interaction, personal conversation, and, in particular, positive feedback. Because Directors often don't give much positive feedback, this may be a stretch, but it is well worth the effort. Remember to be patient, positive, and willing to engage.

Interacting with an Analyst

You are both task-oriented. You are private, emotionally controlled, and base your decisions in logic. The key for you is patience. Analysts' deliberate pace allows them time to gather data, explore options, and process information. Your pace of speech and decision making is naturally fast; so slow things down. With an Analyst, the faster you try to move, the longer things will take—and the less successful you will be. Minimize your use of strong and convictional language which may make you appear pushy or not open to alternatives. Invitational language works best with the Analyst.

Interacting with a Friend

Because you are opposites this relationship requires the most adaptation. Your first task is similar to your task with Analysts— slow your pace of speech and allow for a slightly longer decision making process, and use invitational language. Second, you must meet Friends in their relationship dimension. Friends want a connection with you. Your tendency to get down to business might seem uncaring or impersonal. Spend some time breaking the ice and building rapport by asking the Friend some personal questions and sharing a little about yourself. Even a few minutes of this kind of effort might make the difference in the interaction.

YOU ARE A FRIEND

Interacting with Another Friend

This should be a very natural effort. Be yourself, give what you know you like to receive and all should be fine.

Interacting with an Extrovert

You share a relationship-oriented approach. Your natural strength as a listener, your willingness to receive positive feedback, your comfort in personal connection, and your emotional expressiveness will all match. To adapt to Extroverts, slightly speed up your pace and use language that indicates confidence.

Interacting with an Analyst

Because you both fall on the indirect side of the model, your pace of speech, patience in decision making, good listening skills, and choice of words will mesh. Analysts may not want a personal connection. Asking personal questions and spending too much time trying to break the ice could make Analysts feel uncomfortable, intruded upon, and frustrated by your lack of focus. Remember to emphasize logic and reason.

Interacting with a Director

Because you share neither dimension of the model, you likely will have a hard time being successful if you stay in your natural style. Your ideal interaction is based on relaxation and connection; the Director is looking for fast results. Quicken the pace of your speech and decision making. Directors are focused on accomplishing tasks rather than building relationships. This is not to say that Directors aren't interested in getting to know you; however, they usually prefer to wait until they've satisfied their needs or at least until they are confident things are in motion. Toward the end, let Directors lead the way in personal conversations and use language with conviction, so they can see you are confident but not cocky.

YOU ARE AN EXTROVERT

Interacting with Another Extrovert

Because you are a match, you will understand each other well. Remember the customer should be the focus of the conversation and the one doing most of the talking. As an Extrovert be aware of your own need to be the center of attention and realize that it's important for your fellow Extroverts to feel as though the focus is on them, not you.

Interacting with a Friend

This also tends to be a natural fit, because of your similarities in relationship orientation. Your emotionally expressive nature, charisma, and ease of connecting with others will serve you well. Slow your pace, use your listening skills, and make sure the Friend does most of the talking. Finally, be aware that your enthusiastic nature and use of convictional language might appear pushy or coercive. By using invitational language you avoid these risks.

Interacting with a Director

You are both more direct so your pace and assertive language will match. Remember that Directors value time and efficiency and like speaking with people who are concise. As an Extrovert you enjoy a good chat which can quickly frustrate Directors. Although your natural tendency may be to build rapport, it's important initially to make the task the priority. Directors appreciate a more emotionally controlled and formal approach, so beware of using overdramatic body language and emotional expressions. Finally, make sure that you emphasize logic and data.

Interacting with an Analyst

Because this style is directly opposite to yours, treating an Analyst as you want to be treated won't work. As an Extrovert, your strengths are your contagious passion and enthusiasm for people. When interacting with Analysts, however, these strengths can actually hinder success and may result in your intention not matching your impact. Therefore temper your enthusiasm to meet Analysts in their comfort zone. This approach creates trust, interest, and commitment. Slow your speech, listen patiently, and use invitational language to communicate. Demonstrate calm and restrained body language. Use fact and logic, rather than feelings or instinct. The more detail you can provide the better. Lastly Analysts like to reduce risk, so try to provide data that demonstrates security and predictability.

16

CULTURAL TELLS

Most of us have heard the word *culture,* and used it in a variety of ways. It's such a fundamental concept that terms have developed around it, such as *subculture, counterculture,* and *culture shock.* At its most basic, a culture consists of a group of people who share common traits. This includes a *language:* vocabulary, jargon, and expressions they understand in a similar way. Every culture has *norms*—things that are considered normal and expected. It also elevates certain *values* above others, and considers specific behaviors unacceptable or *taboo.*

Why are we focusing on culture? Remember, our objective is to follow the Platinum Rule and treat people the way they want to be treated. As we learned in Chapter 6, the foundation of the Platinum Rule is the ability to quickly and accurately read people. Anything that helps us predict our customer's behavior will help us determine how he or she wants to be approached, how we can make that customer feel comfortable, and how to create a positive relationship with him or her.

As culture consists of patterns of behavior, knowing key aspects of a customer's culture can show us the dos and don'ts of providing excellent customer service.

The second part of the Platinum Rule involves adjusting our own behavior to others' expectations. Just as we need to know our own style and comfort zone before we can adapt to others, we must understand our own cultural patterns before we can adjust to a customer's norms.

We can all benefit from knowing ourselves better, and our cultural heritage and patterns are important keys to this understanding. Additionally, many customer service employees routinely deal with people from different cultures. It is unrealistic to think that you can become knowledgeable about every single culture. However, if your company tends to have many customers from a few specific cultures, it is advantageous and realistic to become knowledgeable of these cultures. For example, if you work in South Brooklyn, near Brighton Beach, you probably have many customers with Russian backgrounds. Other examples include the Mexican culture in Southern California, the Cuban population in Miami, the Japanese culture in Thailand, and the emerging Chinese culture in Mexico. There are also significant cultural differences within the United States.

THE IMPORTANCE OF CULTURE

Cultural studies are no longer the sole province of academic anthropologists. Businesses have invested in a range of activities to become more astute in this area. Some businesses have hired cultural anthropologists to study their specific corporate culture. Using the same tools they would in the field, anthropologists help the company better understand its norms and values. Other companies send key employees to cross-cultural training before starting assignments. Nancy Adler has studied cultural differences and how they impact business relationships. For example, she observed the amount of silence in conversations around the world. She found that the most silence was likely to occur in Japan and the least in Brazil. (In fact, she found that there was, on average, no silence in Brazilian conversations.) (Adler, 1997). This type of information can be helpful in navigating a new culture.

In trying to understand culture's impact on behavior, we are always balancing two truths about human beings. The first is that people are creatures of habit. Our culture exerts a powerful influence on our habits because of four factors: genetics, modeling, rewards, and punishments.

1. *Genetics.* No one has resolved the nature-nurture debate, but people from the same culture may share genetic material.
2. *Modeling.* Educators call this *observational learning.* Most of us learned more by watching people around us than we learned in a classroom. Culture simultaneously restricts the range of behaviors we see and repeats the behaviors to which we are exposed.
3. *Rewards.* Culture has the power to shape our behavior through signs of approval, status, or love when we act in a way our culture deems appropriate.
4. *Punishments.* As we will see when we discuss cultural taboos, a culture can send signals of disapproval, shame, guilt, and even withdraw love in response to certain behaviors.

In these ways, culture exerts a powerful influence on our personalities even though we are not always aware of it. We shouldn't underestimate the power of culture.

The second truth that balances the impact of culture is that trend is not destiny when it comes to habits. Even though we each come from a specific background we all have the capacity to change, learn, and grow. We can, with effort, develop new behaviors.

CULTURAL STEREOTYPES

Given these two truths about human beings, it's important to use all the knowledge we can acquire about someone's culture to strengthen our relationship with the customer but also to avoid some of the traps of stereotyping. Remember that while people are strongly influenced by their cultures, within every culture there is a broad spectrum of personalities and behaviors.

Positive Stereotyping

Viewing someone through the lens of culture is a form of stereotyping. This can be effective and useful if we follow two important guidelines:

1. Remember that any "facts" we know about a particular culture are generalizations that may apply to a greater or lesser degree to specific individuals.
2. Use these generalizations as starting points to anticipate behavior and preferences with the goal of making an interaction more supportive, respectful, and productive.

Negative Stereotyping

The potentially negative side of making cultural generalizations is that each person is unique, and you may make mistakes because someone doesn't fit your assumptions. A second type of negative stereotyping occurs when we perceive a customer's culture as inferior to our own and it affects the way we treat him or her. We learned in Chapter 2 that our negative self-talk about customers also influences our treatment of them. Notice if your negative self-talk involves particular cultures. You are possibly overgeneralizing based on a few people you've met from those cultures. You also may not understand enough about their culture to interpret their behavior correctly. Whatever the case, we encourage you to use more helpful self-talk when dealing with customers from these particular cultures.

CULTURAL MARKERS

Because not many of us have time to pursue a graduate degree in cultural anthropology or take six months off to travel the world, we are going to give you a crash course in culture. First we describe four cultural markers (language, norms, values, and taboos) that we recommend you pay attention to when exposed to a culture different than your own.

Language

Because communication is at the core of customer service, it's important to study how a culture or subculture uses words or expressions. If someone from Brooklyn reacts to your statement by saying "Unbelievable!" it doesn't mean he doesn't believe you. If a Japanese woman nods her head and says "Hai, hai," (Yes, yes), it may not mean she is agreeing with you—she might just be acknowledging your statement.

Cultural Norms

We all have a sense of what is considered normal behavior, but cultural anthropologists caution us that we tend to define normality for all people based on what is normal for our culture. This is called an ethnocentric bias. When we see the same behaviors, body language, facial expressions, and reactions repeated over many years, we create a concept of what is normal and expected. These norms, however, may only be true for our culture, not for all people. If we fall into the ethnocentric trap, we judge people based on our specific cultural definition of normality. For example, in almost all cross-cultural studies the United States ranks close to the top in individual competitiveness. If someone from the United States thinks that this attitude is normal for everyone he or she may misunderstand and misjudge someone from a more cooperative, group-oriented culture.

Experts often advise, "If you want to be an expert in someone else's culture, study your own first." We need to know our culture's norms because they are often the filters through which we view others. For many of us, being immersed in a culture our whole lives means we don't notice some of its basic traits. People often say, "You never really understand your culture until you leave it." Only by seeing other norms can you see your own more accurately.

These norms can include very specific behaviors such as eye contact, touch, distance between people when conversing, and subjects that can be discussed in public. At one point Marty was in a German train station and went to a kiosk for some chicken before boarding. Anticipating a messy meal, he started to grab a few napkins, but the proprietor stopped him, saying he was taking too many. Even after hearing his rationale, the kiosk owner said, "It's not normal."

Cultural Values

Many values can be important in a culture: patriotism, family, self-reliance, modesty, confidence, toughness, altruism, financial success, frugality, enjoyment, physical attractiveness, or religious piety. A specific culture can't value all these traits equally especially as some of them conflict with one another. In fact, cultures do value some traits more than others. People who exhibit these valued traits are highly regarded and widely admired. A culture's history often highlights examples of people putting these values into practice. If you want to learn about a culture—whether it belongs to a country, a region, or an organization—it's important to find out what core values it holds in high esteem.

Cultural Taboos

A taboo is a behavior that is forbidden or provokes strong negative reactions in a certain culture. Breaking a taboo can be a quick way to alienate a customer forever. While the behavior may seem normal to you; without you knowing it, you might have offended your customer. You may have grown up in a culture in which, for example, it is normal to brag about your accomplishments. This behavior is unacceptable, however, in parts of the world, including Thailand, Japan, and even parts of the United States. Some people grow up in egalitarian societies such as Australia or the United States, where equality is a highly praised societal trait. Other societies emphasize respect and deference to authority figures or elder members. These societies would consider it offensive to treat these people informally or as equals.

Some cultures are more tactile than others. In a culture in which touching and kissing is taboo, exhibiting this behavior can alienate a customer. Privacy also varies between cultures. A French executive told us that in his country, the university one attends can reveal a great deal about one's status and potential for career success. For that reason, many French executives consider this information private. Imagine their reaction if they visited the United States and a friendly coworker asked, "So, where did you go to school?"

BASIC CULTURAL BEHAVIORS

At this point you may be thinking, "There is so much to learn, and so many things I might miss." First, consider our motto: "improvement, not perfection." Congratulate yourself for making a sincere effort to learn about yourself and others. Also, remember you probably only need to learn about one to three cultures that represent sizeable numbers of your customers.

Some basic aspects of behavior have an immediate impact on face-to-face discussions. We recommend that you learn these essentials about the main cultures you are likely to encounter. They include the following:

- Eye contact
  - Too little
  - Too much
- Touching
- Personal space

No matter with what culture you interact, these behaviors will factor into how comfortable customers feel. We will highlight some different cultural expectations in these areas so you can start the conversation positively. If you are unsure of a culture's norms or are dealing with a customer from a culture you don't know much about, watch the customer's behavior in these three areas and try to match it.

Eye Contact

The amount of eye contact we make and the time we spend looking at others is determined by what our culture deems normal and acceptable. That's why when we are with people from our neighborhood or culture we often don't even think about eye contact. However if we just do what feels normal to us when talking to someone with different expectations we run certain risks.

Too much eye contact. If you are used to making a lot of eye contact there are two risks. First, a person accustomed to making less eye contact will experience negative emotions when being given too much eye contact. For example, an older Japanese person might perceive you as aggressive and find your gaze oppressive. The second risk is that in some societies, such as in the Middle East, men and women who aren't related to each other make little or no eye contact. If you make too much eye contact or gaze too long at someone of the opposite sex in this kind of culture you may embarrass or provoke the person.

Michael Argyle, an expert in social psychology and nonverbal communications, recommends that in all situations, it is good practice to notice and then to mirror the degree of eye contact your customer displays. (Argyle, Dean, September, 1965)

Too little eye contact. If you make less eye contact than your customer expects he may question your confidence or honesty. For example, many parents in the United States tell their children to look people in the eye when speaking to them—an illustration of the teaching of a cultural norm.

Touching

Allan and Barbara Pease, authors of *The Definitive Book of Body Language* (2006), have researched the amount of touching that is considered normal in 42 different countries. They found an extraordinary range of behavior. Observing people eating lunch in outdoor cafes, they recorded 220 touches per hour in Italy, and 142 per hour in France. At the other end of the spectrum, in London, there was often no touching. Other high-touch countries include Greece, Spain, Puerto Rico, and Brazil. Of course, differences exist within countries. Even in France you see much more touching in Marseilles, which is on the Mediterranean Sea, than in British-influenced Bordeaux. The Peases found that low-touch countries included Germany, Japan, England, New Zealand, and several Scandinavian countries.

It's important to pay attention to this aspect of behavior. Because touching can be taboo in some countries, and lack of touching can be seen as unfriendly and standoffish in others.

Personal Space

Edward Hall is considered a pioneer in cultural studies. He found that a person's sense of territory is culturally determined (1966). Each of us sees a certain area around us as an extension of our body. If someone invades our space by getting closer to us than we consider normal we become uncomfortable, scared, or angry. On the other hand, if we come from a culture where people stand closer to each other, such as in Southern European countries, and someone keeps a distance, we perceive that person as unfriendly or think she doesn't like us. Again, the best advice is to study your customer's preference so you can get into her comfort zone.

DIMENSIONS OF DIFFERENCE

Many of Marty's 1,500 assignments as an executive coach involved Americans working outside the United States, or foreigners working for a multinational corporation. He has studied the key dimensions of difference that are likely to appear between cultures. You can benefit from this research. As with the basic dimensions just discussed, we strongly recommend that you try and gather information regarding these additional dimensions if difference for main cultures you anticipate interacting with. Below we describe each dimension and the cultural tells that help you identify a person's place within it. You can also use this list to learn from your coworkers and customers about their cultures.

The five main dimensions of difference between cultures are:

1. Private versus open
2. Polite versus direct
3. Modest versus self-promoting
4. Hierarchical versus egalitarian
5. More silence versus less silence

These dimensions will help you identify the key values, norms, and taboos of customers. These dimensions won't tell you everything, but they cover the basic issues that can come up in customer service situations. As you read about them, please remember that improving customer service is a combination of focusing on others and learning about yourself. When you understand the range of behavior and the tells associated with each dimension try to place yourself, as well as others, somewhere along the continuum. We conclude each description with a few examples of cities, countries, and regions that we have found correspond with the two side of dimension.

Private versus Open

People who value privacy have a strong sense of what should and should not be discussed. This could include certain subjects (religion, money, among others), personal information, or inner feelings. This sense of privacy can extend to their friends and family, so you can imagine how they might approach you, a stranger, in a customer service situation. As well as not sharing information about themselves, private people avoid asking you anything they think is too personal.

How do you recognize a private person? These people may be formal and businesslike, and stick to the task at hand. They probably will keep their distance from you, and prefer a structured setting for discussions. If you happen to ask something they consider to be none of your business, you will often see them pull back slightly and give you a curt response. They may seem irritated or uncomfortable if you reveal things about yourself that they consider irrelevant. Your best approach is to be businesslike and focused. Let them ask the questions, or if you have questions, explain why you need the information.

Open people enjoy discussing many aspects of their lives and feelings. These customers exhibit many tells, especially in the hospitality, gaming, or tourism industries. They sometimes tell you more personal information than you want to know about them. In turn they may ask you about yourself, and then begin a discussion about things you have in common. They want you to be interested in them and open about yourself. Stay within the boundaries of what you consider appropriate, but be engaged.

Here are some examples of private cultures versus more open ones.

Private	Open
Scandinavian countries	Brazil
Japan	Italy
England	French Canada

Polite versus Direct

Many parts of the world, as well as regions of the United States, put a high value on being polite. People in these areas thank you often and show signs of appreciation. They are considerate of and attentive to other people's needs, and also have a tendency to apologize for their own behavior or ask permission to do something. Obviously, you want to match their politeness. If they see you engage in what they consider rude behavior, they react negatively, but may be too polite to tell you.

Polite	Direct
Thailand	Hong Kong
Japan	Israel
Midwest/southern U.S.	New York
New Zealand	Northern Holland

Some cultures, however, don't value politeness much at all. People of these cultures won't be afraid to tell you that you are wrong, have made a mistake, or that your clothes don't match. These folks can actually get uncomfortable with people they regard as too polite, because they are unsure what the other person is really thinking. At the extreme end of the scale are people who engage in teasing and sarcasm. When dealing with these people, be direct, but don't match their criticisms or teasing. Instead, use the customer service vocabulary that we have discussed.

Modest versus Self-Promoting

Modest societies usually have a religious or ethical foundation that puts a high value on humility. In these societies it's a cultural taboo to call attention to yourself or portray yourself as better than others. Sayings in these societies include warnings such as, "The nail that stands up is the one that gets hammered," and "The tall poppy is the one that gets cut." People might also discount their own ability and show discomfort with compliments. In this culture, any bragging on your part will trigger a negative reaction.

Societies that value confidence and personal achievement often foster more competitive environments. There may be a daily struggle for attention and status. Fortunately, in terms of tells, people from these societies give you clues readily and frequently: Their clothing, jewelry, or cars are often expensive and showy. They quickly find a way to tell you about their accomplishments or reputation. Sometimes they also like to name-drop.

Modest	Self-promoting
Thailand	Hong Kong
Japan	Israel
Midwest/southern U.S.	New York
New Zealnd	Northern Holland

Unlike customers on the other end of the scale, these folks love compliments and recognition. We suggest you catch them doing something right. You will notice that when you give them compliments, their faces light up and their energy level increases. It may take time, but let them tell you about their successes. Not only will this make them feel good, but also will give you insight into what matters to them and motivates them.

Hierarchical versus Egalitarian

In a hierarchical culture, respect and power are given to certain people, and these people are used to being treated in a deferential way. Age, seniority, or knowledge may determine the pecking order. Someone from this kind of culture who occupies a superior position will be used to being treated with respect. People acknowledge this person's superiority and are willing to accept roles of service in relation to him or her.

A high-status person may be used to people serving him, for example. He may give orders and expect quick reactions. At other times he may ignore someone he perceives as being in a service role. He certainly doesn't expect to be treated as an equal by a customer service employee. In his culture, service workers might be expected to use honorific language, bow, or touch their toes. If you are working in the United States, your company is not expecting you to go to extremes, but try to remember that this person believes it is your role to serve him.

Hierarchical	Egalitarian
India	United States
Japan	Australia
Saudi Arabia	Canada

In egalitarian societies, people grow up valuing equality and fairness. The prevalent thinking is that respect must be earned and not simply given to an authority figure or an elder. People from these types of societies are more likely to treat you as a person fulfilling a service role, rather than as a servant.

More Silence versus Less Silence

As we mentioned earlier, Nancy Adler specifically studied this aspect of cultural difference. This may not seem as important an issue as modesty versus self-promotion or hierarchy versus egalitarianism, but customer service interactions are conversations, and silence or the lack of it can be a big factor.

In cultures with more silence, people take time to think and reflect before responding, or keep quiet until they have something to say. They are used to being with others and being quiet. In this situation, most people from the United States feel uncomfortable and want to fill the silence. Instead, speak less, give your partner more time to think, be patient, and remember that this is the norm in his or her culture.

People in less silent cultures are used to highly interactive, engaging conversations featuring frequent interruptions, quick responses, and more than one person speaking at once. In some conversations, the person who ends up as the listener is simply the first one who has to take a breath. In these situations, stay engaged and respond quickly to questions and comments.

More silence	Less silence
Japan	Brazil
Thailand	Italy
	Greece

Mid-Range Behaviors

To help you understand the range of each dimension of difference we have described the extremes. Not all cultures will be extreme and not all people from a particular culture will behave a certain way all the time. In dealing with people from less extreme or more familiar cultures we recommend using the Golden and Platinum Rules. With people at each end of the scale, however, cultural tells can often give you great insight into this particular customer's norms, values, and taboos.

LEARNING ABOUT CULTURES

There are several ways to learn more about your customers' cultural patterns. The most costly is by trial and error—learning the hard way through making mistakes. We don't recommend this method; we've learned that when customers have negative experiences, they often won't come back, and therefore don't give us feedback. It's better to ask a coworker or a friendly customer for information. Reading books by culture experts, reading travel guides, watching travel shows, and watching movies from other countries accelerate your learning. If you want to make sure that you don't use any offensive gestures or tells, read Roger Axtell's *Gestures: Dos and Taboos of Body Language* (1997).

We encourage you to be curious and open-minded about different cultures, because, as you can see, you will also learn more about yourself.

17

THIRD-PARTY TELLS

The main theme of the chapters in Part II is that tells give you potentially useful information, starting with the idea that "people will tell you how to sell them." This rich flow of data becomes our guide to customers' expectations and needs.

Because millions of people around the world fulfill customer service roles, there are many types of interactions. A majority of situations involve meeting or talking on the phone with a customer who is a total stranger, and whom you may not see again. For these situations, we have highlighted in-the-moment, communication style, and cultural tells that you can notice even during short conversations. Obviously if your interaction lasts longer or you have repeat customers, not only can you notice more tells, but you can also have more confidence in the cues you pick up.

Lots of people in customer service roles have long-term, in-depth relationships with their customers, especially in these fields:

- Consulting (financial planning, engineering, construction, marketing, strategy, information technology)

- Services (law, architecture, landscaping, accounting)
- Sales (ongoing client servicing/client relations after a sale is made)

Many corporate roles also involve consulting with internal clients—for example, human resources, training, information technology, or strategic planning. These positions also require you to be able to zero in on patterns, anticipate needs, and predict reactions.

Another type of information is also available if you are in a field that cultivates long-term customer relationships. We call this set of data *third-party tells*. The term refers to useful information from others (the third party) who know your customer or client. You may be in a network of people that includes your client or your client's organization. With the goals of maintaining positive relationships, exceeding customer expectations, and discovering what people really want, we show you how to get the most out of third-party tells.

AVOID GOSSIPING

Because using third-party tells involves talking about others who are not present, it's important that we touch on the subject of gossip. Our goal is to direct your attention to acquiring information ethically and achieving a win-win outcome for you, your organization, and your customer. Toward this objective, let's distinguish positive behaviors from ones to avoid, which can be categorized as negative gossip.

If we are discussing a client or customer with a third party, it is important to avoid certain subjects.

- Don't discuss private aspects of a client's life that have no relevance to your working relationship.
- Avoid bad-mouthing a client, or criticizing behavior that doesn't apply to your customer service role.

- Use good verbal discipline; don't repeat rumors, and gently discourage others from sharing them with you.

INFORMATION GATHERING

When preparing to meet a customer for the first time, it's ethical and savvy to try to obtain as much useful information as possible from your network. Of course, when you meet him or her, you can also observe tells and add this information to your customer profile.

Even if you have learned about a customer before meeting him or her, or have had regular experience with that customer, it's still important to gather new information from your network occasionally. Modern businesses are rapidly changing organisms and it's a good bet that bosses, roles, structures, or priorities may have shifted. A third party can give you a heads-up about the changes and their implications for your client.

We tackle specifics about types of information later in this chapter. In general, you are looking for information to help you do the following:

- Provide excellent service.
- Learn how your client likes to be approached.
- Know what makes him upset and how to avoid it (land mines).
- Identify the client's core values.

If you work in the corporate world, you may have heard the saying, "You can discover where the land mines are in two ways: One is to have someone point them out so that you can avoid them; the other way is to step on one yourself." If you work inside a corporate headquarters, you can sometimes step on a land mine and survive. However in customer service situations, you may never get a second chance.

NETWORKING

Many books have been written on this subject, so we'll discuss only certain aspects of this vital behavior. Networks are crucial to success if you are trying to climb the corporate ladder. If you work in client services or customer relations you now also know that creating and maintaining your network will give you key, timely information. It can also provide an even more valuable service: feedback. Remember, research shows that many disappointed clients do not give feedback. When you sense something went wrong, but your client doesn't tell you directly, your network may be able to help you pinpoint what you should have done differently.

Networking Tips

- *Start early.* The day you need a network, it is too late to build one.
- *Think wide.* People often leave situations for a variety of reasons. If your network is too narrow, it may disappear overnight.
- *Think wired-in.* Almost everyone is useful in some way, but some people are much more valuable than others. In every organization, some people tend to know a lot of useful, accurate information. Make sure the people in your network are wired-in.
- *Think quid pro quo.* You won't get very far in network-building if you approach people with this type of attitude: "I read this book about the value of networks, so would you like to be in mine…" Networks are maintained because they are mutually useful, not one-sided. Think about what's in it for the person you want in your network, so you can make it a win-win relationship.

THE PROCESS OF ACQUIRING
THIRD-PARTY INFORMATION

Your relationship-building and networking skills will hopefully create the trust and credibility that makes it easier for people to be open with you. At this point, your listening skills will determine the amount of valuable information you acquire.

1. Listen Carefully for Stories or Anecdotes about Your Client

Example 1.
Third Party: "Well, I think I did something right this morning."
You: "What did you do?"
Third Party: "I guess it's what I didn't do. Jim [the client] asked me a tough question at this morning's meeting and I wasn't sure of the answer. I didn't want to look stupid in front of him and the team, but I decided not to try to bluff my way through it. I said, 'Jim, I don't know the answer, but I'll get you the precise figure in 24 hours.' Then I held my breath, but I saw a big smile on his face and he said, 'That's fine. I appreciate your honesty.'"

Example 2.
Third Party: "Boy, Sally learned the hard way about how important deadlines are to Susan [the client]."
You: "What happened?"
Third Party: "Sally committed to Susan to complete the report by Friday at noon. She didn't think it was a big deal if she got it to her later Friday afternoon. At 12:30, Susan was at Sally's desk with fire in her eyes. I hope she never looks at me that way."

Example 3.
Third Party: "I wish Paco had asked me for advice before he made that presentation to David [the client]."
You: "How come?"

Third Party: "Paco thought he had some practical ideas to improve results, but he didn't realize that David would see them as small ideas. He called Paco's ideas *incremental*. That's not a compliment from someone who gave a speech on the 'tyranny of incrementalism.'"

If you have a good network, you hear many varieties of these anecdotes involving your clients. Listen carefully and extract the lessons about what matters to your client.

2. Use Open-Ended Questions

Before you demonstrate your curiosity about the client and use open-ended questions with the people in your network, it's important to establish the rationale for your approach. Always emphasize that the reason you want to learn about the client is to meet or exceed expectations, treat him or her the way he or she wants to be treated, and continue to add value. Remember what you learned about open-ended questions from Chapter 3: We want to find out what is most important to our clients, and discover their optimal preferred approach to working with people. The only difference is that now we are asking these questions about the client to a third party. We'll get to the subjects on which you most want information in the next section, "Types of Third-Party Information."

3. Be on the Alert for Changes, and How They Will Affect Your Client

For a variety of reasons, many related to advances in technology, the rate of change is increasing in almost all industries. This means that while it's still useful to acquire basic information about clients through noticing tells, recognizing their styles, or asking a third party, your information may not be complete. Change in your client's world usually means that his or her focus will be different and he or she will inevitably reprioritize what is important.

For example, external changes regarding consumers, competition, or the economy, or internal changes regarding people, management, or organizational structures, can influence a client in the following ways:

- Short-term versus long-term thinking
- Appetite for risk
- Sense of security
- Optimism/pessimism
- Cost consciousness

While networking, be sure to listen for and/or ask questions about recent internal and external changes.

TYPES OF THIRD-PARTY INFORMATION

In-the-Moment, Communication Style, and Cultural Tells

We don't want to reinvent the wheel if we don't have to. If your third party has read this book or is knowledgeable about tells, just ask that person what he or she has observed about your customer in these areas. For someone who won't know what you mean when you talk about these categories, simply describe some of the behaviors that you have learned are important. For example, use your knowledge of style to ask if a particular likes to get right down to business, or if she prefers to spend time getting to know people first. The third party may know about your customer's cultural background, for example, if she has parents who immigrated from another culture, or if she worked or lived in another country. You have to prime the pump a little more, but you can still guide the third party to make some useful observations.

This process also increases your third party's awareness of and sensitivity to these issues. Don't be surprised if the next time you talk to him or her, the person provides even more insights.

Core Values

In Chapter 16, you learned that we all have a variety of values, some of which we describe as core values because of the emotional weight they hold. If you connect with someone's core values, you are well on your way to forging a bond. If you go against a core value, you may never recover. That's why it is so important to find out as much as possible about these areas in advance.

Examples include the following:

- *Integrity*. Everyone says this is a core value, but some people define it in specific terms and react strongly to perceived violations of those terms. They may get upset about an employee putting a hotel movie on his expense account, or making a personal phone call from the office.
- *Fairness*. Again, this is a trait we all agree is important, but some people have a more finely tuned sense of fairness. It could stem from family behavior, sibling relationships, or being part of a disadvantaged ethnic group. For whatever reason, this person has an emotional reaction when he or she perceives unfair treatment.
- *Spending money*. Most psychologists agree that money is a very emotional issue, and the source of many marital disputes. This is because people come into marriages with deep-seated feelings about money that are hard to change. Your clients and customers are the same way, and they aren't married to you. Some are very concerned about being overcharged. Some are very frugal and look down on people who they feel don't know the difference between a luxury and a necessity. Some will judge your status by your clothes and watch.

Other examples of core values include work ethic, teamwork, and candor. Finding out about your customers' core values should be a high priority.

Communication Preferences

In addition to communication style, anything you can learn about communication preferences will be very valuable. With all the options people have for receiving information (voicemail, cell phones, faxes, BlackBerrys, e-mail, instant messaging, pagers, and so on), it's impossible to predict the mode a customer will want you to use. Most people are under steady time pressure, and they can get quite frustrated if they don't receive information in a speedy, and—for them—user-friendly way. Try to learn about their preferred mode and frequency. In addition, it is crucial to learn what they regard as confidential and how they expect you to handle this information.

Boundaries and Role Clarity

Lack of role clarity and blurry boundaries are major sources of conflict within teams. If you have an ongoing relationship with a client, you constitute a type of team; clearly defined roles and specific boundaries often prevent misunderstanding. At minimum, try to find out if the client has strong boundaries and roles that he or she wants people to adhere to, or if he or she is more relaxed and open to you suggesting ideas that go beyond your normal role.

Tolerance for Disagreement

This is a key quality to study, because you can make two types of mistakes. If the client values constructive confrontation and candor, yet you avoid any differences and never give an alternate point of view, your credibility will diminish. If the customer is polite and nonconfrontational, he or she might take offense if you are too direct and blunt.

Decision Making

At some point in your working relationship with a client, you will be actively involved in the decision-making process. The most challenging part of this process is that people approach decision making in so many different ways.

- Are they intuitive and/or impulsive, or do they want to follow a systematic process?
- What is their tolerance for risk; are they afraid of making a mistake?
- Do they worry more about the cost of being wrong, or the cost of being slow?
- Do they seek input from you and others, then try to reach a consensus? Or do they keep their own counsel and decide independently?

WHAT CLIENTS REVEAL WHEN THEY TALK ABOUT A THIRD PARTY

There is another version of third party tells that we have found yields the most useful and reliable information about a client. This is the insight you can gain when your client discusses his or her likes, dislikes, and preferences regarding other people. Here is our rule for learning in these situations:

When a client gives you feedback about a third party, he may be giving you some accurate information about the third party, but he is *definitely* giving you accurate information about *himself*.

When clients make these comments about others, they are giving you an inside peek at their values and preferences. Here is an example that illustrates the power of this technique, especially when different clients discuss the same person.

Client A talks to you about Keisha: "You know, I like how she handles herself at meetings. She doesn't talk just to hear herself speak. I see her listening attentively, and then she gives her opinion at the right time."

Client B talks to you about Keisha: "I really expected more from her. She isn't the kind of visible leader we need. She's too polite. I wonder how confident she really is."

These clients are talking about Keisha in part, but we hope you see that they are also talking about themselves.

- *What do people notice about others?* We all notice different things when we observe people. What we notice is indicative of our own values, likes, and dislikes.
- *What do we choose to focus on?* Client A focused on listening skills and timing. Client B focused on participation or the lack thereof.
- *We use our own scorecard to evaluate others.* Even when Client A and Client B observed similar behaviors, such as politeness and modesty, they evaluated Keisha differently. That preference or dislike gives you insight into the most important thing to know about clients: their scorecard for what they value in others.

When you are with your clients, listen for the many comments they make about others.

- He is too quiet.
- I don't see any intensity; where is the fire in the belly?
- She is too full of herself.
- That's the kind of person I like. He is moderately ambitious. He knows he has to pay his dues before he moves ahead.
- I can't stand these people. They bring me problems without giving me solutions.

- Wow, is she focused. She never goes off on tangents. We get closure before we move on.

We encourage you to learn about every type of information described in this chapter, even if only through observation. Our repeated experience is that if you can learn any of it through third-party tells, you will start the customer relationship on solid ground and avoid mistakes that can permanently derail it.

CHANGING CUSTOMER SERVICE CULTURE

18

CREATING
A CUSTOMER SERVICE
CULTURE

The final chapter of this book is for readers who occupy supervisory, managerial, or executive positions in the customer service industry. You are responsible for creating an environment, or culture, that supports and sustains positive behavior toward customers.

We can continue our discussion about culture by examining how to create a business in which excellent customer service is the norm. We are aware of culture's power to reward and reinforce behavior, thereby creating norms, values, language, and taboos. Now let's see how we can increase the chances that the skills of *Customer Tells* become widespread.

If we simply rely on individual effort some employees will turn out to be self-starters who are committed to learning and improvement. Exposing them to a book or a training seminar may be enough. If the messages are clear and compelling, the skills are easy to learn and use, and there is an opportunity to practice them and see their advantages, then these employees will change their behavior. Unfortunately, there may not be enough "early adapters" to change the culture.

The keys to comprehensive culture change are:

* Achieving critical mass
* Inspect what you expect
* Consequences for leaders
* Hiring criteria
* Customer insights

ACHIEVING CRITICAL MASS

For new behaviors and values to permeate a culture, you need to achieve a critical mass of employees who embrace the change. Most experts who study this phenomenon say 30 to 40 percent of your employees must be on board with change for it to really take root. If you fall below critical mass you run several risks. It's hard for people to change their behavior. For many of us, the path of least resistance is to keep doing what we are doing. It's very easy to slide back into old behaviors, particularly under stress. This is why when you institute a change management project, many of your employees will stay on the fence while only a few will fight it. If you don't reach a critical mass of employees they may see the new program as a flavor of the month that will soon fade away, and they won't make the effort to change.

Let's discuss what you can do as a leader in your organization to reach critical mass in the area of excellent customer service.

Modeling

When we teach Customer Tells seminars to frontline employees, they sometimes say, "My superior could use this class." This is often followed by a question: "Will senior management receive this training?" These remarks reveal employees' desire that their supervisors display the same behaviors they themselves are learning. There are two main side effects of training employees:

1. *Increased awareness and sensitivity.* When people read or learn about skills such as listening, positive attitude, responsiveness, respectful behavior, and emotional management, they focus most on two elements: their own behavior and how they are treated. Often they think about the skills (or lack thereof) of their peers, supervisors, and sometimes friends and family, in those areas. For example, after attending training sessions dealing with good listening, people are much more aware of nonlistening behaviors and may get upset about issues they previously tolerated. They will be extra conscious of how they are being treated. As a result, although they may not give direct, immediate feedback, they might react strongly if a supervisor fails to use the skills of *Customer Tells.*

2. *Raising the bar.* As well as raising awareness, knowledge of these skills also raises expectations and standards. If senior management members endorse the training program and espouse its values, participants will start to scrutinize their behavior and expect them to "walk the talk." A crucial part of the total Customer Tells program is that supervisors consistently model its skills. Just as we don't expect frontline employees (or ourselves) to demonstrate Customer Tells skills perfectly, we also shouldn't have that expectation of supervisors. Instead, they should aim to master and internalize the skills and apply them as best they can when handling customers and employees. If they are willing to do this the organization will derive huge benefits.

Reinforcement

In our seminars we try to demonstrate the skills, not just talk about them. If supervisors do this too they create an extended virtual classroom that reinforces the desired behaviors. They are leading and teaching at the same time. When supervisors use the skills with employees there are two positive outcomes: Not only do the employees get to see the Customer Tells program in action, but they also feel its positive impact.

Credibility

Remember, your employees are always checking to see if you are truly embracing these values or just giving them lip service. When you choose to demonstrate a flexible approach and adapt your style to other people you become a credible voice. You also eliminate employees' most common excuse for delivering poor service: "Why should I treat the customer this way? This is not how I'm treated."

INSPECT WHAT YOU EXPECT

These four words sum up our approach to performance management in a family or business. Essentially, it means you need to follow up to make sure your expectations are being met. Many actions accompany these words, but they all emphasize the fact that others often watch your behavior to see which issues especially matter to you. Imagine a parent telling a child, "I expect you to put away your toys after you play with them," but provides no consequences if the kid refuses to do so. Some children will put their toys away because you expect it or because they have already developed a sense of responsibility. A much larger percentage will watch your actions not your words. If you don't inspect what you expect they may assume that the issue doesn't matter to you and that there are no real consequences of noncompliance.

The two basic components of inspect what you expect are:

1. Catch people doing things right
2. Give corrective feedback

Catch People Doing Things Right

This phrase refers to observing employees' behavior and delivering some form of positive reinforcement when you see them doing things right.

Positive feedback. Comments that acknowledge employees' behavior show employees that you are paying attention and you care. While they may welcome general statements such as "Great job," or "I like how you are treating our guests," you can have an even greater impact by using "camera-check" positive feedback. This refers to feedback so specific that a camera could see or hear the behavior you are describing. For example, instead of saying, "You seemed to handle that situation very well," a supervisor might say, "I couldn't hear every word of your conversation with the guest, but I observed that you didn't interrupt him even when he was talking for a while." Camera-check feedback lets the supervisor praise a specific skill. The employee knows exactly what he did right and therefore is much more likely to repeat the behavior.

Rewards and recognition. Experts have found that rewards motivate us as adults almost as much as they did in elementary school. Remember the mileage your first-grade teacher got out of gold stars and stickers? Most people are wired to respond to rewards such as money and prizes, and there is a multi-billion-dollar industry designed around providing incentives to employees. Approval and recognition also matter. Recognizing employees' achievements, publishing company newsletters about positive experiences or customer feedback, and giving out awards can sometimes mean more than a cash sum that can be spent and forgotten.

Analyze success. When asked, "Do you learn more in life from failure or success?" most people answer, "failure." It doesn't have to be that way. Most people learn more from their failures because they spend much more time analyzing them. When we have setbacks or make mistakes we experience a varying level of pain or loss. Often we want to understand what went wrong and figure out how to avoid repeating the mistake in the future.

What happens when we get things right? How often do we have the same motivation, as we do with failure, to get to the bottom of why things went well? Most people rarely analyze their successes, which means they miss a valuable lesson: Success has within it a template that can be replicated and shared. True professionals are not only good they also know why they are good.

Just because you were successful once doesn't mean you will remember to do things the same way next time around. Toward the end of one training seminar Marty conducted, the eldest salesperson in the room stood up and said, "I want all you young people to listen to Marty. These skills work. In fact, I used to do everything he is talking about."

We all can drift away from effective behavior if we don't nail down exactly what we need to replicate. It's a good individual practice to analyze your success. After a customer interaction has gone well take some time to focus on what you did that contributed to the positive result. Analyzing success can become a standard organizational practice for your entire company. Peter Early of Wynn Resorts is one executive who has implemented this idea. He collects stories of excellent customer service at Wynn Properties, and then distributes them internally for all Wynn employees to read. Because these memos focus on the specific steps employees took to achieve these results they serve as positive feedback and recognition as well as analyzing success.

Corrective Feedback

Skillfully executed corrective feedback is extremely hard to find. Remember: You are the expert on your inside but other people are the experts on your outside. If we make a mistake, we may not see exactly what went wrong. A vague sense that the interaction didn't go well won't help you pinpoint what you should do differently next time. To improve as customer service employees or leaders we need timely corrective feedback from people with whom we work closely with. Unfortunately, if it isn't delivered with some skill, it can lead to defensiveness and indifference instead of learning and motivation.

Years ago one of the authors was living near Columbus, Ohio, when Jack Nicklaus was playing in his memorial tournament. Jack played poorly for the first two rounds, and then came roaring back in the last two to win the title. Later, he attributed his dramatic turnaround to a phone call from his high-school coach after the second round. "Jack, I'm watching you on TV," the coach told him. "Remember what you used to do with your thumb in high school? Well, you're doing it again." (Columbus Dispatch, 1984)

This feedback was useful and timely. Jack Nicklaus was number one in the world that year, but he didn't notice his thumb misplacement until his coach pointed it out. It wouldn't have had the same impact if the coach said, "Jack, you are playing terribly. You almost missed the cut in your own tournament."

Do's and don'ts of corrective feedback. As we mentioned above, if corrections are not handled with care they can have the opposite effect, making an employee less interested in improving his or her performance.

- *Timing.* Jack's coach timed his feedback perfectly. The action was fresh in Jack's mind and he could put the guidance into practice immediately. If we wait too long to give feedback everybody's memory of what happened can get fuzzy.
- *Setting.* Nicklaus received his feedback in private. In fact, if he hadn't shared it with a reporter no one else would have known. Almost everyone is less defensive and more receptive if you have the patience and discipline to deliver criticism one-on-one. This can be a challenge in a hotel, casino, restaurant, or showroom floor.

- *Your emotional state.* What you learned about being on tilt or going limbic applies doubly here. Our goal is for corrective feedback to help not punish. If you correct someone when you are upset, you may come off as tactless. Remember when we are upset we are inclined to:
  - Exaggerate ("always" or "never")
  - Speak louder
  - Curse or name-call more
  - Listen less

Try to give corrective feedback when you are calm or only mildly upset.

Number of issues. Some people's idea of giving feedback is to hit you with everything but the kitchen sink. It might seem as if they are saying, "While we are discussing all the mistakes you make with customers, let me tell you about..." This can cause people to shut down, thus limiting learning. A better approach is to be timely and deal with only a few issues at a time.

Camera check. While a camera check enhances positive feedback, it's downright essential to corrective feedback. Jack Nicklaus's coach used camera-check feedback. He didn't talk about Jack's game,or even his swing; that wouldn't have given Jack the information necessary to improve. The coach talked about the position of his thumb.

Our goal when describing customer tells skills was to be as specific as possible, even down to which words to use. We hope that as supervisors and managers you can leverage these specifics when you give camera-check feedback. Instead of making a general statement like, "You didn't communicate well with that customer," tell your employee exactly what he said and how to say it differently.

CONSEQUENCES FOR LEADERS

Inspecting what you expect increases the chances that your employees will demonstrate the desired behaviors. It's also necessary to inspect supervisors, managers, and higher positions.

Does customer service excellence matter to the company? If so it should be featured on the company "scorecard." This can include measuring customer satisfaction levels; giving high-performing teams and leaders raises, bonuses, and promotions; and withholding rewards from those who aren't demonstrating improvement.

HIRING CRITERIA

Our entire professional careers have been devoted to training. We are strong believers in the ability of individuals to acquire new skills and create better results. However we also agree that the quickest way to improve your organization is to hire and retain talented people. Employees with the right attitudes consistently get the most out of training. *Customer Tells* highlights the mental, emotional, and communication skills that make an excellent customer service employee and can inspire companies to check for those skills when hiring. If a potential employee displays a positive attitude, self-talk and listening skills, flexibility, emotional self-management, and the ability to read tells, hiring her will accelerate the creation of the service culture you are looking for.

CUSTOMER INSIGHTS

Entire departments of corporations are devoted to discovering the most current consumer tastes and trends. Marketing executives conduct analyses and assemble focus groups. The information they gather then shapes product development and presentation. We are not suggesting that companies abandon these efforts, but we do recommend augmenting them with data that their customer service employees obtain. Years ago, there was a saying in sales training: "Your salespeople are potentially your best market researchers." Salespeople confront reality in the marketplace every day. They can see what's working and what isn't, what's important to their customers and what they do not care about. They may even be able to spot trends and discover what the competition is doing.

Similarly, the ability to read tells gives your frontline employees vital information about their customers. They can pick up interest, note dissatisfaction, and record preferences. Equipped with open-ended questions and an ear for side comments, they can gather many insights into customers and competitors.

Here is how to capture this information and convert it into useful planning and strategic thinking.

- *Customer service employees.* Give them open-ended questions they should ask, based on your industry. Chapter 3 has some good examples of effective open-ended questions.
- *Gathering insight.* To spot trends you need a broad view, so it is essential that supervisors regularly collect insights and observations from the people on their teams.
- *Strategic thinking and planning.* If senior management can devote part of a meeting, once a month, to brainstorm about customer insight and the implications of change the organization will become highly responsive to customers and won't be likely to have blind spots about changes in the marketplace.

Your customer service employees can give you information that cannot always be obtained by other means. Focus group feedback primarily reflects what customers say. Research in several fields indicates that what people say they will do or what they want can differ from their actual behavior. Anthropology is founded on the principle and practice of observing and recording behavior. If an anthropologist wanted to learn more about customers' likes, dislikes, and reactions, she would observe them in the field rather than relying solely on interviews and surveys.

Tom Kelley, the CEO of the award-winning innovation consulting firm IDEO, talks about a key role employees can play in generating customer insights. In his book *The Ten Faces of Innovation* (Kelley, Littman, 2005), he names one role the "Anthropologist," and describes the importance of observing people engaged in activities. The powerful insights gained from direct observation can be translated into improved or innovative products. Your customer service employees using their new observational skills can play the role of Anthropologist. If you can capture their insights and add them to your customer feedback surveys and focus groups you may have a more complete picture of customer trends.

The following are some examples from our clients:

- A hotel valet-parking attendant was chatting with a taxi driver. The driver mentioned that several guests had remarked in his cab about the poor quality of customer service they had received at the hotel. This information eventually was passed along to senior management and led to training that improved the service level.
- Employees heard from several customers that even though the company's advertising emphasized certain benefits, what they appreciated most about the product was the time it saved. The marketing department was made aware of this data and after some consumer insight research, modified their advertising strategy.
- A customer relations employee developed a trusting relationship with a client. The client opened up to her about what the competition was doing better than her company. This competitive insight was shared, checked out, and was ultimately very useful to the company in its strategic planning process.

CONCLUSION

We hope that we have achieved our goals in sharing our ideas about customer tells.

- *Core values.* Skills and behaviors can be used in a variety of ways. It's important to us that we've conveyed that all the skills you've learned can be used with sincerity and the ultimate goal of meeting someone's needs.
- *Life skills.* Now that you have read about all the skills that combine to help you deliver exceptional service, we hope you have even more perspective on why we call them life skills. Our experience tells us that they may benefit you in all your relationships.
- *Trend is not destiny.* Self-talk, listening, vocabulary, style, and reading tells are all based on habits. We can build new habits with practice and feedback. So start small, practice as much as you can, and get a feedback buddy to monitor your progress.

Speaking of feedback, we would love to get yours. Any comments, questions, or suggestions are very much appreciated. This is how we improve our seminars and writing.

You can contact us with your feedback, or obtain more information about our seminars, coaching, or consulting at:

Optimum Associates, LLC
www.optimumassociates.com
ben@optimumassociates.com

Adamson, Allen. 2006, May 2. "ADVERTISING; Nowadays, It's All Yours, Mine or Ours." *New York Times,* page C1.

Adler, Nancy. 1997. *International Dimensions of Organizational Behavior.* Cincinnati, OH: South-Western College Publishing.

Alessandra, Tony, and Michael J. O'Connor. 1996. *The Platinum Rule: Discover the Four Basic Business Personalities—and How They Can Lead You to Success.* New York: Warner Books.

Anderson, Jenny. 2006, August 11. "Hedge Fund Manager Who Plays His Cards Right." *New York Times,* page C1.

Argyle, Michael, and Janet Dean. 1965, September. "Eye-Contact, Distance and Affiliation." *Sociometry,* pages 289–304.

Axtell, Roger. 1997. *Gestures: Dos and Taboos of Body Language.* Hoboken, NJ: John Wiley & Sons.

Brizendine, Louann. 2006. *The Female Brain.* New York: Morgan Road Books.

Butler, Pamela. 1991. *Talking to Yourself: Learning the Language of Self-Affirmation.* New York: HarperCollins.

Cammack, John. Interview with the authors. September 12, 2006.

Caro, Mike. 2003. *Mike Caro's Book of Tells.* New York: Cardoza.

Casey, Phil. 2000, November 16. "Media Life Proving a Struggle for Woods." *The Birmingham Post* (England).

Dubos, Rene. From a talk given at the Conference on Technological Change and the Human Environment, California Institute of Technology, October 19–21, 1971.

Fitzgerald, Tom. 2006, August 13. "Tipping Points." *San Francisco Chronicle,* page C1.

Goleman, Daniel. 2006. *Social Intelligence: The New Science of Human Relationships.* New York: Bantam.

Hall, Edward T. 1966. *The Hidden Dimension.* New York: Anchor Books.

Hallowell, Edward M. 2006. *Crazy Busy: Overstretched, Overbooked, and About to Snap! Strategies for Coping in a World Gone ADD.* New York: Ballantine.

Kelley, Tom, and Jonathan Littman. 2005. *The Ten Faces of Innovation: IDEO's Strategies for Defeating the Devil's Advocate and Driving Creativity Throughout Your Organization.* New York: Currency.

Kroft, Steve. Television interview. 2004, November 21. "Carrey: 'Life Is Too Beautiful'." *60 Minutes.* Produced by CBS Worldwide Inc.

Lazarus, David. 2006, August 16. "Data Theft May Hurt Workers." *San Francisco Chronicle,* page C1.

———. 2006, August 13. "At Your Service, Right?" *San Francisco Chronicle,* page F1.

McLuhan, Marshall. 1969. *Counterblast.* New York: Harcourt, Brace & World, Inc.

Nalywayko, Maria. Interview with the authors. July 17, 2006.

Navarro, Joe, with Marvin Karlins. 2006. *Read 'Em and Reap: A Career FBI Agent's Guide to Decoding Poker Tells.* New York: HarperCollins.

Nicklaus, Jack. Anecdote, Interview with the *Columbus Dispatch.* 1984.

Nusbaum, Howard. 2006, July 22. "Analog Acoustic Expression in Speech Communication." *Journal of Memory and Language,* pages 167–177.

Pease, Allan and Barbara. 2006. *The Definitive Book of Body Language.* New York: Bantam.

Roger, Frederick McFeely. "Mister Rogers' Neighborhood." 1968–2001. Produced by Family Communications Inc. and WQED Pittsburgh.

Rogers, Frederick McFeely. Interview with *TV Guide,* 1985.

Runyon, Damon. *New York American,* 1935.

Smith, Gary. 1996, December 23. "The Chosen One." *Sports Illustrated.* http://sportsillustrated.cnn.com/golf/pga/features/tiger/chosen/

Thomas, William I., and Dorothy Thomas. 1929. *The Child in America.* New York: Alfred Knopf.

TVGuide Magazine, October 26, 1996.

Wallace, Mike. Interview with CBS Cares, August 2006. *www.cbs.com/ cbs_cares/depression/wallace.shtml.*

Wikiquote.org, 2006, November 3. A WikiMedia project. Accessed December 6, 2006. *http://en.wikiquote.org/wiki/Damon_Runyon*

Williams, Mark A., and Jason B. Mattingley. 2006, June 6. "Do Angry Men Get Noticed?" *Current Biology,* pages R402–R404.

Wood, Wendy, Leona Tam, and Melissa Guerrero Witt. 2006, June. "Changing Circumstances, Disrupting Habits." *Journal of Personality and Social Psychology,* pages 918–933.

Yang, Jae, and Julie Snider. 2006, April 16. "Best Service Expected at Restaurants." *USA Today,* Money, page 1A.

A

B

C

S

T

Dr. Marty Seldman is corporate trainer, executive coach, and organizational psychologist, specializing in customer service and sales, team-building, conflict resolution, feedback systems and skills, and workshops on building and maintaining trust. With a career spanning over thirty years and around the globe, Marty has trained ten of thousands of executives through his seminars and coached over 1500 executives one-on-one. He is the author of multiple books, including Survival of the Savvy, a Wall Street Journal best-seller, and Super Selling through Self-Talk. Dr. Seldman and his team of John Futterknecht and Ben Sorensen developed the Customer Tells (TM) Training Program and have trained thousands of individuals in organizations across a wide spectrum of industries.

John Futterknecht works as a corporate trainer and executive coach. Having worked in the field for over nine years, John has helped thousands of individuals, both in the United States and internationally, through seminars and one-on-one coaching. He specializes in customer service and sales training, organizational savvy, team-building, conflict resolution, and helping managers provide more effective feedback to employees. John work with Fortune 100 companies as well as non-profit organizations.

Ben Sorensen has excelled in the areas of pharmaceutical sales, financial services and the educational field. Ben has helped thousands of people in corporate and non-profit organizations improve communication skills, resolve conflict, deliver effective customer service, provide more effective feedback to employees, and increase their organizational savvy and success thorough the Customer Tells Training Program and other seminars.